Pr

OUR *One* GREAT
ACT *of* FIDELITY

ALSO BY RONALD ROLHEISER

*Secularity and the Gospel: Being Missionaries to
Our Children*

*Forgotten Among the Lilies: Learning to Love
Beyond Our Fears*

*The Restless Heart: Finding Our Spiritual Home in
Times of Loneliness*

*The Holy Longing: Guidelines for a Christian
Spirituality*

*Against an Infinite Horizon: The Finger of God in
Our Everyday Lives*

*The Shattered Lantern: Rediscovering a Felt
Presence of God*

OUR *One* GREAT ACT *of* FIDELITY

WAITING FOR CHRIST IN THE EUCHARIST

RONALD ROLHEISER

DOUBLEDAY

New York   London   Toronto   Sydney   Auckland

DD

DOUBLEDAY

Published in the United States by Doubleday Religion, an imprint of
the Crown Publishing Group, a division of Random House, Inc.,
New York.
www.crownpublishing.com

DOUBLEDAY and the DD colophon are registered trademarks
of Random House, Inc. ·

Library of Congress Cataloging-in-Publication Data
Rolheiser, Ronald.
Our one great act of fidelity : waiting for Christ in
the Eucharist / Ronald Rolheiser.
p. cm.
Includes bibliographical references.
1. Lord's Supper—Catholic Church. I. Title.
BX2215.3.R65 2011
234'.163—dc22
2011001543

ISBN 978-0-307-88703-0
eISBN 978-0-307-88705-4

Printed in the United States of America

Book design by Lauren Dong
Jacket design by Misa Erder
Jacket photograph by Getty Images

10 9 8 7 6 5 4 3 2 1

First Edition

For the parish community of St. Donatus
in the hill country of Cactus Lake, Saskatchewan,
for raising me in the faith and the Eucharist.
Heartfelt thanks. I carry your birthmark.

CONTENTS

Preface 9

PART ONE. THE EUCHARIST AND THE
INCARNATION 13

1. The Incarnation and the Body of Christ 15
2. The Centrality of the Eucharist to the Christian
    Faith 19
3. The Radical, Shocking, Raw, Physical Character of the
    Eucharist 23

PART TWO. THE MANY DIMENSIONS OF
THE EUCHARIST 27

4. The Eucharist as God's Physical Embrace 31
5. The Eucharist as an Intensification of Our Unity Within
    the Body of Christ: *Totus Christus* 35
6. The Eucharist as the New Manna: God's Daily Bread
    for Us 41
7. The Eucharist as a Meal, as a Celebration of Our
    Health and Joy, and as a Celebration of Our Pain and
    Sorrow 45

8. The Eucharist as a Sacrifice *49*

9. The Eucharist as a Memorial of the Paschal Mystery *57*

10. The Eucharist as Reconciliation—as the New Wine *61*

11. The Eucharist as the Ultimate Invitation to Mature Discipleship—to Wash Each Other's Feet *65*

12. The Eucharist as an Invitation to Justice *73*

13. The Eucharist as a Ritual to Sustain Our Health *77*

14. The Eucharist as a Vigil, as a Communal Rite of Waiting *83*

15. The Eucharist as the Priestly Prayer of Christ *87*

PART THREE. A SPIRITUALITY OF THE EUCHARIST: *RECEIVE, GIVE THANKS, BREAK, SHARE* *95*

PART FOUR. OUR ONE GREAT FIDELITY *119*

PART FIVE. THREE FAMOUS SERMONS ON THE EUCHARIST *123*

Notes and References *137*

This is a very personal book. While it draws upon the insights of various scripture scholars, theologians, and church teachings, in the end, it is mostly a personal statement of how I understand the Eucharist and why, unless some major circumstance prevents me from doing so, I celebrate Eucharist every day. The Eucharist, more so than anything else, is what anchors my life, my prayer, and my discipleship.

And I have a long, rich, mixed tradition in my practice and understanding of the Eucharist:

Mostly, I have Roman Catholic genes, particularly in relationship to the Eucharist. As a child, I was raised in family and community that was deeply Roman Catholic and within which the Eucharist held the central place. Our parish community was too small to have its own priest, and because of this we didn't have the opportunity to go to Eucharist every day. A priest from a neighboring parish would come for mass on Sundays and major feast days and, later on when our country roads became a bit more friendly, on Thursday evenings as well. Our family went to Eucharist whenever we could, and even though we couldn't go to Eucharist every day,

I was raised to believe that daily Eucharist was the ideal. My parents' dream was ultimately to retire to a place where, in their retirement years, they would have the opportunity to go to Eucharist every day. Sadly, they both died before reaching the age of retirement, but I inherited from them and from our parish community the belief that the Eucharist is the centerpiece of Christian practice and that no season of life (and, ideally, no single day) should be lived without it.

At seventeen, I entered the Missionary Oblates of Mary Immaculate and what I had learned from my family was reinforced there. Through eight years of seminary training, daily mass was simply a given, the air we breathed. When I was ordained to the priesthood, I understood, as part of the covenant that a priest makes with the community, that my role as priest contained the promise to habitually (ideally, daily) celebrate the Eucharist as a prayer for the world. I've been ministering as a priest for nearly thirty-seven years and I have kept that promise. Unless circumstances don't allow for it, I celebrate Eucharist every day.

But home is where we start from. Since ordination, through my years of ministry and particularly through my contact with other churches, my understanding of Eucharist has widened. I've never lost the understanding of the Eucharist that my Roman Catholic background gave me; it is still my deepest faith treasure, but, as more and more Protestants and Evangelicals became friends and faith companions, I was introduced to different understandings and practices of the Eucharist and other ways within which to think of the Word and the Eucharist as interrelating. Some of my deepest faith companions now are not Roman Catholics, and they understand certain aspects of the Eucharist differently than I do. One of my godchildren, a niece of whom I am immensely proud, is a Lutheran. I share deeply my faith journey with various Protestant clergy, and some of them share their struggles and journeys with me. I preach to Protestant and Evangelical groups in the same way as I preach to Roman Catholics, and I am empathic toward their faith struggles since those are also my struggles. As I age, my sympathies and my loyalties become more stretched. I'll always be a Roman Catholic, but my faith journey and my heaven now include Protestants, Evangelicals, Jews, Muslims, Buddhists, Hindus, Taoists, and sincere searchers and struggling persons of every sort. The Eucharist is God's banquet table, and in the end, it will manifest the universal salvific will of God who plays no favorites but embraces everyone without discrimination. To deny this is to massively reduce both the scope of Christ's embrace and the meaning of Christian baptism.

This book, because it is deeply personal, will reflect my own particular background: my Roman Catholic upbringing and beliefs, the central place that the Eucharist occupies within that tradition, and my genetic propensity for daily Eucharist. But I hope it will reflect an understanding and a respect for other traditions around the Eucharist and other ways of anchoring faith and searching for intimacy with God and each other. For the times when this understanding and respect is not evident, I apologize in advance. Everyone has biases and blind spots. I freely admit to mine.

Perhaps the simplest rationale for this book is this: The

Eucharist is my major faith-anchor. Whenever I can, I go to Eucharist each day. This book is simply an attempt to explain the reason why—to others no less than to myself.

Ronald Rolheiser
Sarita, Texas

PART ONE

The EUCHARIST *and the*
INCARNATION

1

The INCARNATION *and*
the BODY *of* CHRIST

A story that is familiar to many of us tells of a young girl who woke up one night frightened and disoriented, convinced that there were spooks and monsters around her in the darkness of her room. She ran to her parents' bedroom for safety. Her mother brought her back to her own room, put on a light to show her that there was nothing there, and gently tried to reassure her that she was safe. Then, just before leaving, the mother said to her, "You don't need to be afraid. You aren't alone. God is here in the room with you." The child replied, "I know that God is here with me, but I need someone here who has some skin!"

We are all like that little girl. As human beings we are sensual creatures in the true meaning of that term. We are creatures of the senses: touch, sight, hearing, smell, and taste. Everything that enters us goes through one of those five senses and everything that comes out of us, all communication and expression, comes out through one of those same senses. We are not angels, pure spirits without bodies. We are incarnate spirits, souls that have a body, and so we need things that we can touch, see, hear, taste, and smell.

That is true, too, sometimes especially so, in terms of our relationship to God. A God who is everywhere is, for us, at a certain point, nowhere. We are human. We need a God who has some skin, who can be located, who can somehow be physically touched. And God—who knows human nature, since he created it—respects that need in us and meets us on our own terms. Thus, the central tenet within Christianity, the very thing that defines it, is the belief that, in Christ, God took on concrete flesh and became tangible, physical, someone who can touch and be touched. Indeed the very word *Christ* ultimately means divine reality inside of human flesh.

When John wrote his Gospel, he did not include a Christmas story. In place of the birth of Jesus, he simply wrote, *The word was made flesh and it lives among us.* That single statement defines Christianity. Christianity isn't first and foremost a religion or a set of beliefs. Rather, parallel to the unfolding of the universe itself, it is an ongoing story, the story of God taking on physical flesh in this world, a story that began with the birth of Jesus in Bethlehem and that continues down to this very day. God is still taking on concrete flesh. How?

The mystery of God taking on concrete flesh, which Christians call the incarnation, isn't a simple thirty-three-year incursion of God into human history in the person of Jesus. It's more. God took on flesh in Jesus, but the incarnation didn't end when Jesus ascended back to the Father after his resurrection. The incarnation is still going on. God is still taking on concrete flesh in this world. Where?

In the Christian scriptures, the term *the body of Christ* is used to refer equally to three things: the historical body of Jesus, the body of believers, and the Eucharist. Each of these is referred to *as* the body of Christ. Each *is* the body of Christ. For instance, when Saint Paul refers to either the community of believers or the Eucharist, he never intimates that they are like Jesus, that they replace Jesus, that they are symbolic representations of Jesus, or even that they are a mystical presence of Jesus. Each is equally called the body of Christ, each is that place in our world where God takes on concrete flesh. God still has skin in this world, in the Eucharist and in the community of believers. The incarnation is still going on. The word is still becoming flesh and living among us.

That is the first, and the key, thing that must be said about the Eucharist. Along with the community of believers, the Eucharist is God's physical presence, God's *real* presence in the world. The Eucharist is the place where God continues to take concrete physical flesh just as he once did in the womb of Mary. In the Eucharist, the word continues to become flesh.

2

The CENTRALITY *of the* EUCHARIST
to the CHRISTIAN FAITH

J esus didn't leave us a lot of rituals. He left us his Word[1] and he left us one ritual, the Eucharist. He refers to other rituals such as baptism, and other parts of the Christian scriptures refer to the laying on of hands, to the confessing of sins, and to various kinds of anointing with oil, but Jesus, himself, left us only his Word and the Eucharist.

And it is around these two things, the Word and the Eucharist, that we form community; from these we create church. Historically Roman Catholics and Protestants have differed as to which of these to give the priority. In classical Protestant theology and practice, the Word is central; it is what first and foremost draws us into community. Eucharist might or might not follow. In Roman Catholicism, the Eucharist is given priority and the Word and all the other sacraments are ultimately in support of the Eucharist.[2] In a vast oversimplification, it might be said that Roman Catholics form church around the Eucharist, while seeing the Word as a necessary prelude to and supplement to the Eucharist; whereas Protestants form church around the Word, while seeing the Eucharist as flowing out from that in different ways.

Partly this can be seen simply by walking into either a Roman Catholic or a Protestant church. When you walk into a Protestant church, what is front and center? A pulpit or a lectern, something from which the Word of God is proclaimed and preached. Secondarily there might or might not be an altar, and if there is one, it is generally less centrally situated. The architecture speaks the theology: we gather first and foremost around the Word. The Eucharist takes a secondary place. When you walk into a Roman Catholic church the reverse is true: What is front and center? An altar. Off to one side, far less prominently, is placed a pulpit or a lectern. The message is also clear in the architecture: we gather first and foremost around the Eucharist, and the Word takes second place.

Biblical scholars suggest that this kind of division may have existed already at the time when the Gospels were written. Already then there were major variations among the different communities as to how often the Eucharist was celebrated and what its exact role was in bringing the community together. In either case, however, it was still deemed to be central, the summit to which we are called. Augustine, perhaps the most influential Christian theologian of all time, puts it this way: Jesus didn't leave us the church and from the church we derive the Eucharist; rather, for him, Jesus left us the Eucharist and from the Eucharist we derive the church. The church is in service of the Eucharist, not vice versa. Heaven will be a banquet table. The Eucharist already is that table.

Because of this, Roman Catholics teach that the Eucharist is the source and the summit of all Christian life. However, because it is both source and summit, it gives a mixed message: it is both the sign of our unity and a means of coming to that unity. It is both the end to which all Christians are journeying and, at least partially, the means to get there. This double meaning has been the source of much, and sometimes bitter, debate among the churches in regard to the practice of intercommunion.

3

The RADICAL, SHOCKING, RAW, PHYSICAL CHARACTER of the EUCHARIST

A few years ago Brenda Peterson wrote a book of essays titled *Nature and Other Mothers.*[3] Her first entry is wonderfully named *In Praise of Skin.* In it, she tells how at one point in her life she was afflicted by painful skin rashes. Like the woman with the hemorrhage in the Gospels, she tried every possible doctor, but found no cure. Medication after medication proved ineffective, and eventually the doctors ran out of things to try. The rash always came back.

One day her grandmother assessed her and pronounced a more ancient and accurate diagnosis: "Skin needs to be touched!" Her grandmother then began to give her regular skin massages, and these did what the more sophisticated medicines couldn't do. They cured her.

Peterson's grandmother is right: Skin needs to be touched!

God knows that better than anyone. It's why Jesus gave us the Eucharist. In the Eucharist skin gets touched. The Eucharist isn't abstract, a theological instruction, a creed, a moral precept, a philosophy, or even just an intimate word. It's bodily, an embrace, a kiss, something shockingly physical, the real presence in a deeper way than even the old metaphysics imagined.

For whatever reasons, we tend to shy away from admitting how radically physical the Eucharist actually is. Saint Paul didn't share that fear. For him, the physical communion that takes place in the Eucharist, between us and Christ as well as among ourselves, is as real and radical as sexual union. For example, he argues against sex outside of marriage by saying that our union with Christ and each other in the Body of Christ is so intimate and real that, in effect, we would prostitute that Body if we were to have illicit sex. Strong words, but they are predicated on a very earthy conception of the Eucharist.

The early church followed Paul on this. They understood the Eucharist as so real, so physical, and so intimate that they surrounded it with the same taboos of privacy, reverence, and reticence that we reserve for sexual intimacy. For some centuries the early church had a practice (still partially followed in some present-day church programs) that it called the *Disciplina Arcani*. The discipline tried to guarantee that nobody who was not baptized or fully initiated into the community could participate in the Eucharist (beyond the liturgy of the Word). As well, Christians who were fully initiated were forbidden to speak to outsiders about the Eucharist. The intent of the discipline was not to create a mystique around the Eucharist so as to draw people to it through curiosity. Rather the idea was that the Eucharist is so intimate an act that propriety, respect, and reverence demand non-exhibitionism: you don't make love in public, and you don't talk to outsiders about this kind of intimacy.

We tend to shy away from that kind of talk. Partly that's understandable. It's hard to be comfortable religiously with how Christianity understands the physical and the bodily.

Christianity is without doubt the earthiest of all religions.[4] Unlike most other religions, it doesn't call you out of the physical, out of the body, or out of the world. Rather it tells you that God enters the physical, becomes one with it, blesses it, redeems it, and that there is no reason to escape from it.

Something in that goes against the grain. Christ's relationship to the physical scandalized his contemporaries. "This is intolerable language!" is what the crowds said when Jesus spoke of the physical character of the Eucharist in John's Gospel, and the raw physical character of the Eucharist is still hard for us to accept today. But it's also a wonderful part of Christianity. In the Eucharist, our skin gets touched.

And, given our tensions and loneliness, we need that touch frequently, daily even. The late essayist and novelist Andre Dubus once wrote a wonderful little apologia on why he went to Eucharist regularly, despite the eyebrows that were sometimes raised in the circles he moved in. Here are his words:

> This morning I received the sacrament I still believe in: at seven-fifteen the priest elevated the host, then the chalice, and spoke the words of the ritual, and the bread became flesh, the wine became blood, and minutes later I placed on my tongue the taste of forgiveness and of love that affirmed, perhaps celebrated, my being alive, my

being mortal. This has nothing to do with immortality, with eternity; I love the earth too much to contemplate a life apart from it, although I believe in that life. No, this has to do with mortality and the touch of flesh, and my belief in the sacrament of the Eucharist is simple: without touch, God is a monologue, an idea, a philosophy; he must touch and be touched, the tongue on flesh, and that touch is the result of the monologues, the idea, the philosophies which led to faith; but in the instant of the touch there is no place for thinking, for talking, the silent touch affirms all that, and goes deeper: it affirms the mysteries of love and mortality.[5]

The Eucharist is physical, real, shockingly so.

PART TWO

The MANY DIMENSIONS
of the EUCHARIST

Christians argue a lot about the Eucharist. What does it mean? What should it be called? How often should it be celebrated? Who should be allowed to participate fully?

There are lots of views on the Eucharist. For some it is a meal, for others it is a sacrifice. For some it is a ritual act, sacred and set apart, for others it is a community gathering, the more mess and kids the better. For some it is a deep personal prayer, for others it is a communal worship for the world. For some its very essence is a coming together, a communion, of those united in a single denominational faith, while for others part of its essence is its reaching out, given that it contains an innate imperative to wash the feet of those who are different from ourselves. For some it is a celebration of sorrow, a making present of Christ's suffering, the place where we can break down, for others it is the place to celebrate joy and sing alleluia. For some it is a ritual remembrance, a bringing into the present of the historical events of Jesus' dying, rising, ascending, and sending the Holy Spirit, for others it is a celebration of God's presence with us today. For some it is a celebration of the Last Supper, something to be done less frequently, for others it is God's daily feeding of his people with a new manna, Christ's body, and is something to be done every day. For some it is a celebration of reconciliation, a ritual that forgives and unites, for others unity and reconciliation are preconditions for its proper celebration. For some it is a vigil act, a gathering that is essentially about waiting for something else or someone else to appear, for others it is a celebration of something that is already present and is asking to be received and recognized. For some it is understood to make present the real, physical body of Christ, for others it is understood to make Christ present in a real but spiritual way. Some call it the Lord's Supper, some call it the Eucharist, some call it the Mass. Some celebrate it once a year, some celebrate it four times a year, some celebrate it every Sunday, and some celebrate it every day. Who's right?

In truth, the Eucharist is all of these things, and more. It is like a finely cut diamond twirling in the sun, every turn giving off a different sparkle. It is multivalent, carrying different layers of meaning, some of them in paradoxical tension with others. There is, even in scripture, no single theology of the Eucharist, but instead there are various complementary theologies of the Eucharist.

For instance, we already see variations among the apostolic communities as to how they understood the Eucharist, what it should be called, and how often it should be celebrated. Some early communities called it the Lord's Supper, connected its meaning very much to the commemoration of the Last Supper, and celebrated it less frequently, whereas the apostolic community that formed around John connected its theology and practice very much to the concept of God feeding his people daily with manna, and they celebrated it every day, given that we need sustenance daily.

As well, we see some of its paradoxical elements right within its central symbols, the bread and the wine. Both are paradoxical: Bread is both a symbol of joy, togetherness, health, and achievement (the smell of fresh bread and the primal beauty of a loaf of bread) even as it is made up of broken kernels of wheat that had to be crushed in their individuality and be baked in fire to become that bread. Wine is both a festive drink, the drink of celebration, of wedding, even as it is the product of crushed grapes and represents the blood of Jesus and the blood and suffering of all that is crushed in our world and in our lives.

How does one put this all together? By letting the Eucharist be patient with us.

During my theological training, I took three major courses on the Eucharist and, afterwards, decided that I didn't understand the Eucharist. But the fault was not in the courses, which were excellent. The fault, which is not a fault at all, lies in the richness of the Eucharist itself. In the end, it defies not just theology professors, but metaphysics, phenomenology, and language itself. There is no adequate explanation of the Eucharist for the same reason that, in the end, there is no adequate explanation for love, for embrace, and for the reception of life and spirit through touch. Certain realities take us beyond language because that is their very purpose. They do what words cannot do. They also are beyond what we can neatly nail down in our understanding.

And that is true of the Eucharist. It is has multiple layers and multiple faces.

4

The EUCHARIST *as* GOD'S PHYSICAL EMBRACE

There's a story told of a young Jewish boy named Mordechai who refused to go to school. When he was six years old, his mother took him to school, but he cried and protested all the way and, immediately after she left, ran back home. She brought him back to school and this scenario played itself out for several days. He refused to stay in school. His parents tried to reason with him, arguing that he, like all children, must now go to school. But to no avail. His parents then tried the age-old trick of applying an appropriate combination of bribes and threats. This too had no effect.

Finally, in desperation they went to their rabbi and explained the situation to him. The rabbi simply said, "If the boy won't listen to words, bring him to me." They brought him into the rabbi's study. The rabbi said not a word. He simply picked up the boy and held him to his heart for a long time. Then, still without a word, he set him down. What words couldn't accomplish, a silent embrace did. Mordechai not only began willingly to go to school, he went on to be-come a great scholar and a rabbi.

Among other things, what this parable expresses won-derfully is how the Eucharist works. In it, God physically embraces us. Indeed that is what all sacraments are, God's physical embrace. Words, as we know, have a relative power. In critical situations they often fail us. When this happens, we have still another language, the language of ritual. The most ancient and primal ritual of all is the ritual of physical em-brace. It can say and do what words cannot.

Jesus acted on this. For most of his ministry, he used words. Through words, he tried to bring us God's consolation, chal-lenge, and strength. His words, like all words, had a certain power. Indeed, his words stirred hearts, healed people, and af-fected conversions. But, powerful though they were, in time they too became inadequate. Something more was needed. So on the night before his death, having exhausted what he could do with words, Jesus went beyond them. He gave us the Eucharist, his physical embrace, his kiss, a ritual within which he holds us to his heart.

To my mind, that is the best understanding there is of Eu-charist. Within both my undergraduate and graduate theo-logical training, I took long courses on the Eucharist. In the end, these didn't explain the Eucharist to me, not because they weren't good, but because the Eucharist, like a kiss, needs no explanation and has no explanation. If someone were to write a four-hundred-page book titled *The Metaphysics of a Kiss*, it would not deserve a readership. Kisses just work, their inner dynamics need no metaphysical elaboration.

The Eucharist is God's kiss. As Andre Dubus so succinctly puts it, "Without the Eucharist, God becomes a monologue."[6] He's right. We need more than words, we need to be physically touched. This is what happens in the Eucharist and it is why the Eucharist, and every other Christian sacrament, always has some tangible, physical element to it—a laying on of hands, a consuming of bread and wine, an immersion in water, an anointing with oil. An embrace needs to be physical, not only something imagined.

G. K. Chesterton once wrote, "There comes a time, usually late in the afternoon, when the little child tires of playing policeman and robbers. It's then that he begins to torment the cat!"[7] Mothers with young children are only too familiar with this late-afternoon hour and its particular dynamic. There comes an hour, usually just before supper, when a child's energy is low, when it is tired and whining, and when the mother has exhausted both her patience and her repertoire of warnings: "Leave that alone! Don't do that!" The child, tense and miserable, is clinging to her leg. At that point she knows what she has to do. She picks up the child. Touch, not word, is what's needed. In her arms, the child grows calm and tension leaves its body.

That's an image for the Eucharist. We are that tense, overwrought child, perennially tormenting the cat. There comes a point, even with God, when words aren't enough. God has to pick us up, like a mother her child. Physical embrace is what's needed. Skin needs to be touched. God knows that. It's why Jesus gave us the Eucharist.

5

The EUCHARIST as an INTENSIFICATION of Our UNITY Within the BODY of CHRIST: TOTUS CHRISTUS

There is a story told about a Jewish farmer who, because he was careless, had to spend a Sabbath day in his field. Preoccupied with his work, he had let the sun go down without going home. Now, being a pious believer, he was not allowed to travel until sunset the next day. So he spent the day in the field, by himself, missing both the Seder meal with his family and the services at the synagogue. When he finally did return home the next evening, he was met by an irate wife and an equally upset rabbi. The rabbi chided him for his carelessness and asked him, "What did you do in the field by yourself all day? Did you at least pray?"

"Rabbi," the farmer answered, "I'm not a very smart man and I don't know many prayers. All the prayers I knew, I said in five minutes. What I did the rest of the day was simply recite the alphabet. I left it up to God to make some words out of all those letters."

We leave it to God to make the words out of the alphabet of our lives. There are few better ways to describe how the Eucharist works in terms of forming us into one heart in Christ. The Eucharist, as we know, is meant to form us into one body in a way that takes us beyond the differences and divisions of personality, ideology, theology, gender, ethnicity, history, social status, preoccupation, privatized agenda, and jealousy. Often it alone has the power to do this. Why? Why does the Eucharist have such unique power?

The Eucharist creates community in a way that cannot be explained in terms of normal group-process. Only the language of ritual sheds light here. What happens at the Eucharist cannot be extrapolated and explained in terms of simple psychological dynamics. It transcends the purely psychological, as does all powerful ritual process. How? The following analogy might be helpful in trying to understand this.

I entered the Oblate seminary in my late teens as part of a group of nearly fifty young men (with an average age of under twenty-five). We were housed in one small, overcrowded building that also served us for classrooms, library, cafeteria, and recreation. I lived in that situation, a potential psychological hotbed, for six years, and, overall, it was a wonderful experience. Despite our differences in background and personality and our youthful immaturities, we basically got on quite well with each other. Very few left the seminary, in those years, over relational difficulties with other seminarians.

However, one of the linchpins within our daily program was something we called *Oraison*. It worked this way: For half an hour each morning and for another half hour each evening we would sit together, all of us, in complete silence in the chapel. No words were exchanged among us, and nothing was expected of anyone except his silent presence. Looking back now, I see that this particular practice of sitting together in silence, in prayer, for an hour each day, did more to bring us together and keep us together than did all the community-building exercises we did at other times. It created a ritual container that held us together in a way that no purely psychological or emotional container ever can. What we had each day was akin to a Quaker silence; we sat together, before God, and asked God to give us something that we could not give to ourselves, namely, community beyond our differences. We asked God to make a single word out of the different letters of our lives.

And it wasn't anything romantic, you can be sure of that! We sat in a chapel, which itself was no aesthetic prize, as a group of immature, young men, and we fought sleep, boredom, our hormones, tiredness, low blood sugar, irritations with each other, full moons, growling stomachs, homesickness, emotional obsessions, scars from our sporting events, and jealousies. This wasn't the holy family, not by a long shot. But it worked, wonderfully. God gave us, daily, something we couldn't give to ourselves, a common heart and common spirit.

The Eucharist works in the same way. It is meant to be an intensification of our unity within the Body of Christ. It is not just the bread and wine that is meant to change and become the body and blood of Christ. There is a famous saying in the writing of the great church Father, Saint Augustine. Whenever he would give communion to someone for the first time, instead of holding up the host and saying, "The Body of Christ," he would hold it up and say, "Receive what you are."

The Eucharist tries, first of all, to change us so that we become what we receive, one body, one community, one heart, and one spirit.

And that is no easy thing to achieve.

There are different kinds of loneliness and different kinds of intimacy. We ache in many places. When I was a young priest, newly ordained and barely beyond the loneliness of adolescence, certain words at the Eucharist touched me deeply. I was young and lonely, and words about being drawn together inside one body and one spirit would incite feelings in me to do with my own loneliness. To become one body in Christ triggered in me an image of an embrace that would put an end to my personal loneliness, my endless aching, and my sexual separateness. Unity in Christ, as I fantasized it then, meant overcoming my own loneliness.

And that is a valid understanding. The Eucharist is an embrace meant to take away personal loneliness, but as we get older, a deeper kind of loneliness can and should begin to obsess us. This deeper loneliness makes us aware how torn and divided is our world and everything and everyone in it. There is a global loneliness that dwarfs private pain.

How separate and divided is our world! We look around us, watch the world news, watch the local news, look at our places of work, our social circles, and even our churches, and we see tension and division everywhere. We are far from being one body and one spirit. So many things, it seems, work to divide us: history, circumstance, background, temperament, ideology, geography, creed, color, and gender. And then there are our personal wounds, jealousies, self-interest, and sin. The world, like a lonely adolescent, aches, too, in its separateness. We live in a world deeply, deeply divided.

And the older I get, the more I despair that there can be a simple solution, or perhaps even a human solution at all, to our divisions. Life slowly teaches us that it is naïve to believe that all we need is simple optimism, goodwill, and an unfailing belief that love will conquer. Love can and will conquer, but it doesn't happen as it does in a Hollywood movie, where two people who really have no business ever being together fall in love and, despite having nothing in common, despite being deeply wounded, despite being immature and selfish, and despite having no shared faith or values, are able to rise above all their differences to sustained embrace and ecstasy, simply because love conquers all.

At a certain point we know that real life doesn't work like that, unless we die in its initial embrace as did Romeo and Juliet. Our differences eventually have their say, both in our personal relationships and in the relationships between countries, cultures, ethnic groups, and religions. At a certain point our differences, like a cancer that cannot be stopped, begin to make themselves felt, and we feel helpless to overcome that.

But realizing this isn't despair. It's the beginning of health. As anyone who has ever fought an addiction knows, the beginning of a return to health lies in the admission of helplessness. It's only when we admit that we can't help ourselves that we can be helped. We see in the Gospels where so many times, immediately after finally grasping a teaching of Jesus, the Apostles react with the words, "If that's true, then it's impossible for us, then there's nothing we can do!" Jesus welcomes that response because in that admission we open ourselves to help, and replies, "It is impossible for you, but nothing is impossible for God!"

Our prayers for unity and intimacy become effective precisely when they issue from this feeling of helplessness, when we ask God to do something for us that we have despaired of doing for ourselves.

As we saw earlier, within Quaker communities people gather and simply sit with each other in silence, asking God to do for them what they cannot do for themselves—namely, give themselves harmony and unity. The silence is an admission of helplessness, of having given up on the naïve notion that we, as human beings, will ever finally find the right words and the right actions to bring about a unity that has forever evaded us.

The Eucharist is such a prayer of helplessness, a prayer for God to give us a unity we cannot give to ourselves. It is not incidental that Jesus instituted it in the hour of his most intense loneliness, when he realized that all the words he had spoken hadn't been enough and that he had no more words to give. When he felt most helpless, he gave us the prayer of helplessness, the Eucharist. Our generation, like every generation before it, senses its helplessness and intuits its need for a messiah from beyond. We cannot heal ourselves and we cannot find the key to overcome our wounds and divisions all on our own. So we must turn our helplessness into a Quaker silence, a Eucharistic prayer that asks God to come and do for us what we cannot do for ourselves: create community. We go to Eucharist for this reason.

6

The EUCHARIST *as the* NEW MANNA:
GOD'S DAILY BREAD *for* US

The Eucharist is meant to be God's regular nourishment for us, daily manna to keep us alive within the desert of our lives.

We get this theology from John's Gospel. The Gospels, as we know, do not have just one theology of the Eucharist. The various communities in the early church each emphasized different things about the Eucharist. John, unlike the other evangelists, does not set the Eucharist so saliently into the context of the Last Supper. He does set it there, but places it in another context as well.

In John's Gospel, where the other Gospels have the institution of the Eucharist at the Last Supper, he has Jesus washing the disciples' feet. Where Matthew, Mark, and Luke have Jesus holding up bread and wine at the Last Supper, John has him holding up a basin and towel. Various scholars, Raymond Brown among them, suggest that John does this because, by the time his Gospel was written, perhaps sixty to seventy years after Jesus died, Christians, not unlike today, were already arguing with each other about the Eucharist: How often should it be celebrated? Who should preside? What is its precise meaning? John, in placing the washing of the feet where the other Evangelists put the words of institution, as we shall see later, is reminding us that washing each other's feet, service to each other and humility before each other, is what the Eucharist is ultimately about. But John also emphasizes another aspect of Eucharist.

While linking the Eucharist to the Last Supper and highlighting that it means service and humility, John also places it into Jesus' discourse on the bread of life. In chapter 6 of his gospel, Jesus says: "Unless you eat the bread of life, you will not have life within you." In speaking of the bread of life, he links it to the manna, the daily feeding that Israel received from God during her years in the desert. During all those years in the desert, manna was Israel's daily food, and often her only food. It had, too, a curious quality. When the Israelites ate it alongside other foods they had procured or brought out of Egypt, it tasted bitter, but if they took manna as their sole food, it tasted sweet. In either case, it was their daily sustenance.

In John's Gospel, Jesus tells us that the Eucharist is the new manna, the new bread from heaven, the new way that God gives us daily sustenance. The Roman Catholic practice of daily Eucharist takes its root here. That is why, too, in Roman Catholic spirituality, unlike much of Protestantism, the Eucharist has not generally been called "the Lord's Supper," since it was understood not as an extraordinary ritual to commemorate the Last Supper, but as an ordinary, ideally daily, ritual to give us sustenance from God.

How does the Eucharist give us daily sustenance? As we saw earlier, the Eucharist nurtures us by giving us God's physical embrace (*the real presence*). God feeds us by physically touching and embracing us. What could be more nurturing to the soul? In Roman Catholic theology and spirituality we are invited to, ideally, receive this touch daily, or at least as often as we practically can. God's touch, the Eucharist, is the new manna, the bread that comes down from heaven.

7

The EUCHARIST *as a* MEAL, *as a* CELEBRATION *of* OUR HEALTH *and* JOY, *and as a* CELEBRATION *of* OUR PAIN AND SORROW

We sometimes forget that Jesus was born in a barn, not a church, and that the God of the Incarnation is as much about kitchen tables as ecclesial altars. God is as much domestic as monastic. This is important to keep in mind as we try to understand the Eucharist. The Eucharist is the body of Christ, a continuation of the Incarnation, and, like Jesus' birth, is meant to bring the divine into concrete, everyday life.

Hence, among its other attributes, the Eucharist is meant simply to be a family meal, a community celebration, a place, like our kitchen tables and living rooms, where we come together to be with each other, to share ordinary life, to celebrate special events with each other, to console and cry with each other when life is full of heartaches, and to be together simply for the sake of being together.

It is not good for the man to be alone. God spoke those words just before creating Eve, and he meant them not just about Adam, the first man, but about every man, woman, child, and creature forever. Nothing is an island, not even a molecule or an atom. Everything is meant to be in relationship. The Eucharist honors that.

When Jesus gave us the Eucharist, he intended it to be a ritual that invites us to come together as a family in every circumstance of our lives. In faith, just as in nature, we are meant to come together with others when we are happy and when we are sad; when the occasion is festive and when it is mundane; when we celebrate new life and when we bury loved ones; when we give ourselves to each other in marriage and when we need reconciliation; when our energy is high and when it is low; when we feel the need for each other and when we want distance from others; and when we have no other reason to be together other than the fact that our nature invites us there.

The Eucharist invites us to gather as family. The very essence of family life is sharing with others both the special and the ordinary moments of life. Families gather together to celebrate occasions: birthdays, weddings, graduations, transitions, illnesses, wakes, and funerals. At these times the atmosphere is more charged, the energy is higher, and there is a clearer sense that this is an occasion that merits our coming together.

But families that sustain community also gather regularly, ideally daily, irrespective of whether there is a special occasion or not. They don't just gather when the energy is good, when everyone is at his or her best, when nobody is bored or angry, and when some occasion merits the effort. They come together regularly, despite tedium, boredom, low en-

ergy, busyness, distractions, and interpersonal tensions, because they recognize, however inchoately, that family life is as
much about sharing the mundane, the distracted, the sports
scores, and the tensions of life as it is about sharing special
and joyous moments. The weekday supper of hot dogs and
beans, wolfed down in twenty minutes with the conversation going no deeper than the sports scores, is not exactly the
same stuff as the fare of the Christmas dinner or the conversation that takes place at a wedding or a funeral, but it is equally
as important in creating family and keeping a family together.
Families are for every day, just as they are for special occasions. So too is the Eucharist.

For a variety of reasons, we have been slow to take this
aspect of the Eucharist seriously, perhaps because its other dimensions seem more sacred. Our reluctance to accept this is
evident in the simple criticism that is made of people who go
to church principally because of its social aspect: "She doesn't
go to church to pray! She just goes for the socializing, for the
chance to talk with others!" That is always voiced as a nega-
tive when, in fact, it is a good reason, among others, to go the
Eucharist. The ritual of the Eucharist was given to us because
we are social in our very makeup. To go to church to socialize
is reason enough to be there.

I wish I had known that as child when I went to church
on special feast days, like Christmas or Easter, and heard the
priest using the word *celebration* to describe our Eucharistic
gathering and never, not even for a second, connecting that
with the much-anticipated family dinner we would be having once we got home from church. I wish, too, that people

would know this when they stay away from church because of boredom or anger or because they feel their presence there is only social and not an act of prayer.

One of the reasons we go to church is to pray, but we go there, too, for the same reason we go to the family table every evening. It's good to be there, no matter what!

8

The EUCHARIST *as* *a* SACRIFICE

For many of us, particularly for Roman Catholics, a key component of the Eucharist is the element of sacrifice. But this isn't easy to understand. What is a sacrifice? What do we mean when we say that we make a sacrifice? We say, for example, *I have sacrificed my career for my children! I sacrifice a lot for my job! Love demands that we make many sacrifices! Sometimes we must sacrifice life itself for the sake of integrity! Christ sacrificed himself for our sins! The Eucharist is a sacrifice!*

From what is common in all these expressions, we can extract the dictionary definition of *sacrifice*: "the surrender of something of value for the sake of something else." That is a good definition, but in terms of its understanding as prayer and as Eucharist, more must be added.

Saint Augustine defined *sacrifice* by saying that it is an act, any act, through which we enter into deeper communion with God and each other, and that the sacrifice opens us to deeper communion by changing and stretching the heart of the one offering it. When we add Augustine's definition to that of the dictionary, we see that sacrifice works this way: *To make a sacrifice is to surrender something out of love, something that is ours and is painful to give away, and to let the pain of that surrender stretch and change our hearts in such a way that we are now more open to communion with God and others.*

The classical example of this is the famous text in scripture where Abraham is asked to sacrifice his son Isaac. What is ultimately behind God's invitation to Abraham to sacrifice Isaac on an altar?

Here are the outer elements of that story: Abraham had longed for a son for many years. Finally, after the situation was humanly hopeless, his wife, Sarah, conceived and they were given a son, Isaac, who is described as Abraham's "only one," his "precious one." But then God invited Abraham to take Isaac and offer him in sacrifice. Abraham, with a heavy heart, agreed to the request and set off with Isaac, carrying wood, fire, and a knife, all the while having to answer his son's questions about why they were not bringing a victim for the sacrifice.

When they arrived at the place of sacrifice, Abraham gathered the wood, lit the fire, bound Isaac, and then raised the knife to kill him. But God intervened, stopped the sacrifice, and gave Abraham a ram instead to offer. The story ends with Abraham walking back to his own land together with Isaac. What is the deep lesson inside this story?

At one level, the lesson is that God does not want human sacrifice, but there is a deeper, more intimate, inner lesson that teaches us something about the innate need inside of us to offer sacrifice. Simply put, the lesson is this: *In order for something to be received as a gift, it must be received twice.* What is implied here?

A gift, by definition, is something that is not deserved but given freely. What is our first impulse when we are given a gift? Our instinctual response is, "I can't take this! I don't deserve this!" In essence, that gesture, that healthy instinctual response, is an attempt to give the gift back to its giver. But, of course, the giver refuses to take the gift back and re-gives it to us with the assurance, "But I want you to have this!" When we receive it the second time, it is now more properly ours because, by trying to give it back, we healthily recognized that it was a gift, unmerited, undeserved.

That is the exact set of dynamics within the story of Abraham offering to sacrifice Isaac. Isaac comes to him as the greatest and most undeserved gift of his life. Abraham's willingness to sacrifice Isaac parallels the instinctual refusal, "I don't deserve this! I cannot accept this!" He offers the gift back to its giver. But the giver, Love itself, stops the gesture and gives the gift the second time. Now Abraham can receive Isaac, without guilt, as gift. When they are walking back home, Isaac is now Abraham's son in a way that he never was before. Abraham had to receive the gift twice by sacrificing it the first time.

That is part of the essence of sacrifice: To properly receive anything, including life itself, requires that we recognize it precisely as gift, as something undeserved. And to do that requires sacrifice, a willingness to give some or the entire gift back to its giver.

We see this as the dynamic underlying the ritual of ancient sacrifice. For example: A farmer would harvest a crop. But before he or his family would eat a even mouthful of it, he would take some of it (the "first fruits") and offer it back to God in the form of a sacrifice, usually by burning it so that that the smoke rising up to the heavens would take some of the crop back to God, whom the farmer saw as the real giver of that crop. After sacrificing some of it in this way, the farmer and his family could now enjoy the rest of it without guilt because, by trying to give it back to its author, they made themselves more aware that it was gift. They can now enjoy it without guilt precisely because, through sacrifice, they have acknowledged it as gift.

That's the inner essence of all sacrifice, whether the sacrificing of a career for the sake of our children or Jesus' sacrifice on the cross. Sacrifice recognizes gift as gift. Like Abraham, it tries to give the gift back to the giver, but the giver stops the sacrifice and gives it back in an even deeper way.

Christians have always seen this same dynamic in the Eucharist: at one level, the priest who stands at the altar at a Eucharist and offers bread and wine to God is, in essence, both Abraham offering Isaac on an altar and the archetypal farmer offering back to God the first fruits of his harvest. And God, in graciousness as always, is stopping the sacrifice and giving the gifts back to us in a deeper way, even as our hearts are being changed by doing this.

But there is a deeper level to this as well, one less easy to explain: this isn't just a wonderful anthropological and religious ritual, though it is that. As Christians, we believe that there is something deeper happening under the surface. We believe that the true priest at the altar is not the officiating minister who is vested and offering the bread and wine, but rather that the real priest is Christ himself and the real elements that are being offered are not bread and wine but the body and blood of Christ, the true first fruits of God's love for us.

In simpler terms, to make a sacrifice is to surrender something out of love, something that is ours and is painful to give away, and to let the pain of that surrender stretch and change our hearts in such a way that we are now more open to communion with God and others. In the Eucharist we reenact Jesus doing that during this life, particularly in how he did it at the time of passion and death. His great act of love in giving over everything, including his very life, in self-surrender, was his sacrifice. He sacrificed as surely and as deeply as any mother who gives up her dream for the sake of her children. And it stretched and opened his heart in a way that let God enter into the world in a way that God had never before been able to enter human history.

The Eucharist, as a ritual, reenacts that sacrifice and invites us to let it stretch and change our hearts as it did Jesus', so that God can, in essence, stop our sacrifice and give back to us, in a deeper way, all that we are trying to offer to God: Isaac, the fruits of our labors, and Jesus himself.

This, of course, isn't easy to understand. Like the real presence, there are no physical or metaphysical categories within which to explain this adequately. But this makes it all the richer. Our failure to have clear categories within which to understand this does not point to some divine magic that is to be received in blind faith, but to something that, precisely because it contains divine elements, cannot be satisfactorily captured in our limited concepts of time and history.

I have searched for years to find a satisfying explanation for how all of this might be explained within our categories of time and history. One of the better explanations that I found is that of C. H. Dodd, a fine biblical scholar. Here is how he describes Jesus' death and its quality of somehow being outside our normal categories of time and history:

There was more here than could be accounted for upon the historical or human level. God was in it. The creative purpose of God is everlastingly at work in this world of his. It meets resistance from the recalcitrant wills of men. If at any point human history should become entirely nonresistant to God, perfectly transparent to his design—then from that point the creative purpose would work with unprecedented power. That is just what the perfect obedience of Jesus effected. Within human nature and human history he established a point of complete nonresistance to the will of God, and complete transparency to his design. As we revert to that moment, it becomes contemporary and we are laid open to the creative energy perpetually working to make man after the image of God. The obedience of Christ is the release of creative power for the perfecting of human life.[8]

A sacrifice made by a great man or woman can alter every aspect of life, for the present and for all that comes after.

Classically, in both the Jewish and Christian scriptures, this has been expressed through the category of remembering in a ritual way so as to "make memorial."

9

The EUCHARIST *as a* MEMORIAL
of the PASCHAL MYSTERY

Once upon a time there was a rabbi who, whenever he wanted God's presence, went to a special place in the woods, lit a fire, said some prayers, and did a dance. Then God would appear to him. When he died, his disciple did the same. If he wanted God's presence, he went to the same spot in the woods, lit the fire, and said the same prayers, but nobody had taught him the dance. It still worked. God appeared. When the disciple died, his own disciple carried on the tradition. If he wanted God's presence, he went to the same spot in the woods and lit the fire. He didn't know the prayers or the dance, but it still worked. God came. Then that disciple died. He also had a disciple. Whenever he wanted God's presence, he, too, went to the same place in the woods, but nobody had taught him how to light the fire or say the prayers or do the dance, but it still worked, God appeared. That disciple, too, eventually died, but he also had a pupil. One day this pupil wanted God's presence. So he searched for the place in the woods, but couldn't find it. And he didn't know how to light the fire or say the prayers or do the dance. All he knew was how to tell the story. But it worked. He discovered that whenever he told the story of how the others had found God, God would appear.

In essence, this story explains how sacred ritual—liturgy—works. Judaism calls this "making zikkaron." Christians call it "making memorial." The idea is that a past event can be remembered, ritually recalled, in such a way that it becomes present again and can be participated in. How is this possible? We have no models in physics, metaphysics, or psychology by which to explain this adequately. Like all ritual, it is beyond simple phenomenology. Ritual is best understood through metaphor, through story, as with the tale just told. God appears whenever certain stories get told.

This idea of making memorial can be helpful in understanding Eucharist. Among other things, the Eucharist is a memorial, a ritual reenactment of Christ's sacrifice of himself for us. Among all the dimensions of the Eucharist, this one, sacrifice, is perhaps the least understood. How is the Eucharist a sacrifice?

As we saw in the previous section, a sacrifice is any act of selflessness, of self-denial, that helps someone else and helps mature the heart of the person making that act. For example, the mother who freely gives up her own dreams of achievement so that her children might have her needed presence during their critical nascent years is making a sacrifice for her children. They will mature more fully and healthily because of it. As Christians we believe that Jesus, not unlike a loving mother, sacrificed his life for us, particularly in the way he gave himself for us in his death. Indeed we believe that we are "saved" by his death, by his sacrifice on Good Friday. But how? How can one person's death help someone else, centuries later?

Properly understood, the Eucharist, as a ritual, gives us another kind of "real presence." It makes present for us the reality of Christ's dying as well as God's response to that, the Resurrection, and invites us to participate in that event. What the Eucharist makes present is not an iconic Christ to be adored or even consumed, but the reality of Christ's dying and rising as an event within which we are invited to participate. Too often this understanding of the Eucharist has been lost, and, as a consequence, we go to Eucharist to receive the person of Christ and to intensify our communion in the body of Christ; both of these reasons are wonderful, valid, and important, but we miss the sense that we are there to participate in the saving event of Christ's death and resurrection, not just to adore or admire it.

But how can we participate in an event now long past in history?

As we saw in the preceding chapter, we have no adequate physics, metaphysics, or theories of time and history to explain that. But we do have a biblical set of categories from both the Jewish and the Christian scriptures. We can make an event from the past present through memorial, through "making *zikkaron*."

When we ritually recount and reenact the story of Jesus' sacrifice (in the Eucharistic prayer, the very heart of liturgy) we experience the "real presence" of the event of Christ's dying and rising. Moreover, that reality is given to us so that we might participate in it. How? We participate in Jesus' sacrifice for us when we, like him, let ourselves be broken down, when we, like him, become selfless. The Eucharist, as sacrifice, invites us to become like the kernels of wheat that make up the bread and the clusters of grapes that make up the wine, broken down and crushed so that we can become part of communal loaf and single cup.

As we saw earlier, occasionally when Saint Augustine was giving the Eucharist to a communicant, instead of saying, "The body of Christ," he would say: "Receive what you are." That puts things correctly. What is supposed to happen at the Eucharist is that we, the congregation, by sacrificing the things that divide us, should become the body and blood of Christ. More so than the bread and wine, we, the people, are meant to be changed, to be transubstantiated.

The Eucharist, as sacrifice, asks us to become the bread of brokenness and the chalice of vulnerability.

10

The EUCHARIST
as RECONCILIATION—
as the NEW WINE

Few persons have understood the Eucharist as deeply as
Saint Augustine. His homilies on it are precious, particularly those he delivered to newly baptized adults who
were receiving the Eucharist for the first time. In one of these
he tells them that their sins are forgiven at the Eucharist:

> Next [at the Eucharist] the Lord's Prayer is said. . . . Why
> is it said before receiving the body and blood of Christ?
> Because perhaps on account of our human fragility our
> minds have imagined something which is not becoming,
> our eyes have seen something which is not decent, or our
> ears heard something which was not fitting. If perhaps
> such things have been kept in because of temptation and
> the fragility of human life, they are washed away by the
> Lord's Prayer at the moment we say "Forgive us our trespasses" so that we can safely approach the sacrament.[9]

According to Augustine, when we stand around the altar
at the Eucharist as a community and sincerely pray the Lord's

Prayer, any sins we have committed are forgiven. The Eucharist is the ultimate sacrament of reconciliation. It is the ancient water of cleansing, now turned into the new wine of reconciliation, that purifies us so that we can enter the house and celebrate. How is this so?

In the second chapter of John's Gospel, we read about the miracle at Cana where Jesus changes water into wine. Too often we see this simply as a gesture of hospitality: when the hosts ran out of wine, Jesus felt sorry for them, and so changed six jugs of water into wine to spare them the embarrassment. Such an interpretation, valid as far as it goes, partly misses the main point. Scripture scholars, Raymond Brown among them, tell us that in the early chapters of John's Gospel there is a strong recurring theme of Jesus replacing the old with the new. That is the case here. He is replacing the old rite of cleansing with something new. What?

Key to grasping the significance of this miracle is the particular jugs of water that got changed into wine. The water that Jesus changed into wine was not the drinking water but the wash water, the water used to ritually cleanse yourself when you entered a house. At the door of every Jewish house stood a series of water jugs, usually six of them, which were kept filled with water. Upon entering a house, you were obliged to first stop and wash your hands and feet, both because they were usually covered with dust and because you were ritually obliged to do this. By washing in this way, you made yourself "clean" so that you could join the household and sit at table with them. What Jesus does at Cana is change this water, used for cleansing, into wine. He replaces the old rite of cleansing with something new—the Eucharist.

The Eucharist is therefore both the sacrament that celebrates unity and the sacrament that cleanses us for it. At the Eucharist our sins are forgiven because to touch Christ is to be healed, even of sin. And we touch Christ, physically, in the Eucharist. But if this is true, if our sins are forgiven in the Eucharist, where does that leave the Catholic sacrament of confession? Is there still a need for explicit confession?

That we can have our sins forgiven by participating in the Eucharist in no way denigrates the need for private confession. The opposite is true: to touch the body of Christ is perhaps the greatest antidote to the rationalizing individualism that precisely tempts us away from explicit confession. A biblical text, the story of the woman with the hemorrhage who touches the hem of Jesus' garment in the hope that her internal bleeding will cease, can be helpful in understanding this. In her encounter with Jesus, we see that there are in fact two moments of healing, the initial touch and a subsequent, explicit, one-to-one conversation. The forgiveness of sins through simply touching the body of Christ in the Eucharist and explicit confession are connected in the same way as that woman's initial touching of Jesus' garment and her explicit exchange with Jesus are related. The person-to-person exchange brings the healing to a fuller moment, a fuller maturity, and a fuller peace. Explicit confession is to the sacrament of reconciliation what an explicit apology is to reconciliation with each other in our daily lives. Actions speak, just as words do, and we can apologize to each other simply by letting our presence speak. But something is left unfinished until an explicit apology is spoken. Mature people apologize, in words as well as in actions. Moreover, as the literature on addictions points out, there can never be a full healing of one's past until one faces, with searing honesty, one's sins and tells them, face to face, to another human being. Explicit, sacramental confession is an indispensable piece within the process of full reconciliation.

However, as both scripture and Augustine assure us, when we stand around an altar at Eucharist and pray the Lord's Prayer, our sins are already forgiven.

11

The EUCHARIST *as the* ULTIMATE INVITATION *to* MATURE DISCIPLESHIP—*to* WASH EACH OTHER'S FEET

In his rather provocative though always interesting autobiography, *Angela's Ashes*, Frank McCourt tells of a confession he once made as a young boy in Limerick, Ireland. His mother has just given birth, and their in-laws from the North have sent five pounds to buy milk for the new baby. But his father, an alcoholic, has taken the money and is drinking it up in the pubs. His mother sends him, a young boy, to find his dad and bring him home. But young Frankie can't find his father. What he finds instead is a drunken sailor in a pub, asleep, with a largely untouched plate of fish and chips in front of him.

Ravenously hungry, he takes the fish and chips outside and eats them. Then, feeling guilty for stealing, he decides he had better go to confession. It's Saturday afternoon and he goes to the Dominican church and confesses to a priest that he stole fish and chips from a drunken man. The priest asks him why he did this, and Frankie answers that he was hungry, that there is not a scrap of food in their house, and that his mother is raging by the fire because his father is drinking away the money meant to buy milk for the new baby. The priest, hearing all this, suddenly becomes quiet. Instead of scolding Frankie and giving him a penance, he does something else:

> I wonder if the priest is asleep because he's very quiet till he says, My child, I sit here, I hear the sins of the poor, I assign the penance. I bestow the absolution. I should be on my knees washing their feet. . . . Go. Pray for me. He blesses me in Latin, talks to himself in English and I wonder what I did to him.[10]

These words wonderfully describe one of the central meanings of the Eucharist. We should be on our knees washing each other's feet because that is precisely what Jesus did at the first Eucharist, and he did it to teach us that the Eucharist is not a private act of devotion, meant to square our debts with God, but a call to, and a grace for, service. The Eucharist is meant to send us out into the world ready to give expression to Christ's hospitality, humility, and self-effacement.

Where do we get such a notion?

This is everywhere evident in the Gospels, though John's Gospel puts it the most clearly. Where the other Gospels have Jesus speaking the words of institution at the Last Supper ("This is my body. This is my blood. Do this in memory of me."), John has Jesus washing the disciples' feet. But, for John, this gesture replaces the words of institution. It specifies what the Eucharist is in fact meant to do—namely, to lead us out of church and into the humble service of others. An old church hymn, often used to send people forth from church, puts it well:

Called from worship into service
Forth in His great name we go
To the child, the youth, the aged
Love in living deeds to show.

This wonderfully expresses what the Eucharist is meant to do. It is a call to move from worship to service, to take the nourishment, the embrace, the kiss, we have just received from God and the community and translate it immediately and directly into loving service of others. To take the Eucharist seriously is to begin to wash the feet of others, especially the feet of the poor and those with whom we struggle most relationally. The Eucharist is both an invitation that invites us and a grace that empowers us to service. And what it invites us to do is to replace distrust with hospitality, pride with humility, and self-interest with self-effacement so as to reverse the world's order of things—wherein the rich get served by the poor and where the first priority is always to keep one's pride intact and one's self-interest protected. The Eucharist invites us to step down from pride, away from self-interest, to turn the mantle of privilege into the apron of service, so as to help reverse the world's order of things wherein pride, status, and self-interest are forever the straws that stir the drink.

It is no accident that, among all the potential scripture texts it might have picked for liturgy on Holy Thursday, the feast that marks the institution of the Eucharist, the church has chosen to use John's account of Jesus washing the feet of his disciples. A splendid choice. Indeed, nothing better expresses the meaning of the Eucharist than does that gesture. But there is still more to this gesture. It embodies an invitation to move to the deepest level of discipleship. What, more specifically, is it asking of us?

Many things divide us: language, race, ethnicity, gender, religion, politics, ideology, culture, personal history, temperament, private wounds, moral judgments. It is hard, in the face of all this, to see people who are different from us as brothers and sisters, as equally important citizens of this world, and as loved and valued by God in the same way we are.

And so we often live in distrust of each other. Sadly, too, we often demonize each other, seeing danger where there is only difference. We then either actively oppose someone or simply steer clear of him or her and caution our loved ones to stay clear as well.

Consequently we live in a world within which various groups stay away from each other: liberals and conservatives, Protestants and Catholics, Jews and Arabs, Arabs and Christians, Muslims and Buddhists, black and white races, pro-life and pro-choice groups, feminists and traditionalists, among others. What we fail to realize is that these differences are really our outer garments, things that in the end are accidental to our real selves. What's meant by this?

We wear more than physical clothing to cover our naked selves; we cover our nakedness, too, with a specific ethnicity, language, religious identity, culture, political affiliation, ideology, set of moral judgments, and a whole gamut of private wounds and indignation. These are in essence our outer garments.

But we also possess a deeper inner garment. Our real substance, identity, and capacity to act with larger hearts, lies underneath. What lies beneath our outer garments?

At the Last Supper, when he is describing Jesus washing the feet of his disciples (in a carefully worded passage), John uses these words: "Jesus knowing that the Father had put everything into his hands, and that he had come from God and was returning to God, got up from the table, took off his outer garments and, taking a towel, wrapped it around his waist; he then poured water into a basin and began to wash his disciples' feet and to wipe them with the towel he was wearing" (John 13: 2–5).

When John is describing Jesus "taking off his outer garment," he means more than just the stripping off of some physical clothing, some outer sash that might have gotten in the way of his stooping down and washing someone's feet. In order to let go of the pride that blocks all human beings from stooping down to wash the feet of someone different from oneself, Jesus had to strip off a lot of outer things (pride, moral judgments, superiority, ideology, and personal dignity) so as to wear only his inner garment.

What was his inner garment? As John poetically describes it, his inner garment was precisely his knowledge that he had come from God, was going back to God, and that therefore all things were possible for him, including his washing the feet of someone whom he already knew had betrayed him.

That is also our true inner garment, the reality that lies deeper beneath our race, gender, religion, language, politics, ideology, and personal history (with all its wounds and false pride). What is most real is that deep down, beneath these other, outer things we nurse the dark memory, the imprint, the brand of love and truth, the inchoate knowledge that, like Jesus, we, too, have come from God, are returning to God, and therefore are capable of doing anything, including loving and washing the feet of someone very different from ourselves. Our inner garment is the image and likeness of God inside of us.

It is only if we realize this that our world can really change because it is only then that liberals and conservatives, pro-life and pro-choice, Catholics and Protestants, Jews and Arabs, Arabs and Christians, black people and white people, men and women, and people wounded in different ways can begin to stop demonizing each other, begin to reach across to each other, begin to feel sympathy for each other, and begin, together, to build for a common good beyond our wounds and differences.

Sometimes in our better moments we already do that. Unfortunately, to have one of our better moments it usually takes a great sadness, a tragedy, or a death. Mostly it is only in the face of mutual helplessness and sorrow, at a funeral, that we are capable of forgetting our differences, putting away our outer garments, and seeing each other as brothers and sisters.

It seems it has never been much different. In the biblical story of Job, we see that it is only when Job is completely down and out, when he is shorn of every outer thing that he can cling to, that he finally sheds his outer garment and utters the timeless line, "Naked I came from my mother's womb, and naked I go back!" We need to be careful what kind of clothing we put on so that the pain of Job is not required to remove it.

One of the deep meanings of the Eucharist is that it invites us to realize that, like Jesus, we, too, have come from God and are going back to God and that therefore all things are possible for us, including a stripping off of the outer garments that so divide us, so that we can begin to wash each other's feet across all lines of difference and division.

12

The EUCHARIST *as an*
INVITATION *to* JUSTICE

When the famous historian Christopher Dawson decided to become a Roman Catholic, his aristocratic mother was distressed, not because she had any aversion to Catholic dogma, but because now her son would, in her words, have to "worship with the help." She was painfully aware that his aristocratic background would no longer set him apart from others or above anyone else. At church he would be just an equal among equals because the Eucharist would strip him of his higher social status.[11]

She intuited correctly. The Eucharist, among other things, calls us to justice, to dissolve the distinction between rich and poor, noble and peasant, aristocrat and servant, both around the Eucharist table itself and afterwards, outside of the church. The Eucharist fulfills what Mary prophesied when she was pregnant with Jesus—namely that, in Jesus, the mighty would be brought down and the lowly would be raised up. It was this very thing that first drew Dorothy Day to Christianity. She noticed that, at the Eucharist, the rich and the poor knelt side by side, all equal at that moment.

Sadly, we often don't take this dimension of the Eucharist seriously. There is a common tendency to think that the practice of justice, especially social justice, is an optional part of being a Christian, something mandated by political correctness rather than by the Gospels. Generally we don't see the call to reach out actively to the poor as something from which we cannot exempt ourselves.

But we are wrong in this. In the Gospels and in the Christian scriptures in general, the call to reach out to the poor and to help create justice in the world is as nonnegotiable as keeping the Commandments and going to church. Indeed, striving for justice must be part of all authentic worship.

In the New Testament, one line out of ten is a direct challenge to reach out to the poor. In Luke's Gospel, we find this in every sixth line. In the Epistle of James, this occurs in every fifth line. The challenge to reach out to the poor and to level the distinction between rich and poor is an integral and non-negotiable part of being a Christian, commanded as strongly as any of the Commandments.

And this challenge is contained in the Eucharist itself: the Eucharistic table calls us to justice, to reach out to the poor. How?

First, by definition, the Eucharistic table is a table of social non-distinction, a place to which the rich and the poor are called to be together beyond all class and status. At the Eucharist there are to be no rich and no poor, only one equal family praying together in a common humanity. In baptism we are all made equal, and for that reason there are no separate worship services for the rich and the poor. Moreover, Saint Paul warns us strongly that when we gather for the Eucharist, the rich should not receive preferential treatment. Indeed, the gospels invite us in the opposite direction. When you hold any banquet, they tell us, we should give preferential treatment to the poor. This is especially true for the Eucharist. The poor should be welcomed in a special way. Why?

Because, among other things, the Eucharist commemorates Jesus' brokenness, his poverty, his body being broken and his blood being poured out. Pierre Teilhard de Chardin expresses this aptly when he suggests that the wine offered at the Eucharist symbolizes precisely the brokenness of the poor:

> In a sense the true substance to be consecrated each day is the world's development during that day—the bread symbolizing appropriately what creation succeeds in producing, the wine (blood) what creation causes to be lost in exhaustion and suffering in the course of that effort.[12]

The Eucharist offers up the tears and blood of the poor and invites us to help alleviate the conditions that produce tears and blood.

And we do that, as a famous church hymn says, by moving "from worship into service." We don't go to the Eucharist only to worship God by expressing our faith and devotion. The Eucharist is not a private devotional prayer, but is rather a communal act of worship that, among other things, calls us to go forth and live out in the world what we celebrate inside of a church: the non-importance of social distinction, the special place that God gives to the tears and blood of the poor, and the nonnegotiable challenge from God to each of us to work at changing the conditions that cause tears and blood. The Eucharist calls us to love tenderly, but, just as strongly, it calls us to act in justice.

To say that Eucharist calls us to justice, and to social justice, is not a statement that takes its origin in political correctness. It takes its origin in Jesus, who, drawing upon the great prophets of old, assures us that the validity of all worship will ultimately be judged by how it affects "widows, orphans, and strangers."

13

The EUCHARIST *as a* RITUAL
TO SUSTAIN OUR HEALTH

A friend of mine, an alcoholic in recovery, likes to explain the dynamics of an Alcoholics Anonymous meeting this way: "It's funny, the meetings are always the same, the exact same things get said over and over again. Everything is totally predictable; everyone, except those who are there for the first time, knows already what will be said. And we're not there to show our best sides to each other. I don't go to an Alcoholics Anonymous meeting to share my talents or to be a nice guy. No, I go because if I don't, I know, and know for sure, that I will start drinking again and eventually destroy myself. It's that simple. I go there to stay alive!"

In a curious, but accurate way, that can also be a description of the Eucharist, at least of one important aspect of it. Among other reasons, we go to the Eucharist to stay alive. The Eucharist is meant to be God's regular nourishment for us, daily manna to keep us alive within the desert of our lives.

Monks have secrets worth knowing. One of these is that a community sustains itself not primarily through novelty, titillation, and high emotion, but through rhythm and routine, through simple, predictable, ritual processes. For example, a wise family will say to itself, "We will all be home at regular times, we will all eat together twice a day, and we will all be together in the living room at least once a day—even if it isn't exciting, even if real feelings aren't shared, even if some are bored, and even if some are protesting that this isn't worthwhile. We will do this because if we don't, we will soon fall apart as a family. To stay together we need regular, straightforward, predictable, daily rituals. We need the manna of daily presence to each other. Otherwise we'll die."

In the Eucharist, God sustains us in just this way.

In a homily at a wedding, Dietrich Bonhoeffer once gave this advice to a young couple: "Today you are young and very much in love and you think that your love can sustain your marriage. It can't. But your marriage can sustain your love."

Love and prayer work the same; the neophyte's mistake is to think that they can be sustained simply through good feelings and good intention, without the help of a ritual-container and a sustaining rhythm. That's naïve, however sincere. Love and prayer can only be sustained through ritual, routine, and rhythm. Why?

What eventually makes us stop praying, John of the Cross says, is simple boredom, tiredness, lack of energy. It's hard, very hard, existentially impossible, to crank up the energy, day in and day out, to pray with real affectivity, real feeling, and real heart. We simply cannot sustain that kind of energy and enthusiasm. We're human beings, limited in our energies, and chronically too tired, dissipated, and torn in various directions to sustain prayer on the basis of feelings. We need something else to help us. What?

Ritual—a rhythm, a routine. Monks have secrets worth knowing, and anyone who has ever been to a monastery knows that monks (who pray often and a lot) sustain themselves in prayer not through feeling, variety, or creativity, but through ritual, rhythm, and routine. Monastic prayer is simple, often rote, has a clear durational expectancy, and is structured so as to allow each monk the freedom to invest himself or hold back, in terms of energy and heart, depending upon his disposition on a given day. That's wise anthropology.

Prayer is like eating. There needs to be a good rhythm between big banquets (high celebration, high aesthetics, lots of time, proper formality) and the everyday family supper (simple, no-frills, short, predictable). A family that tries to eat every meal as if it were a banquet soon finds that most of its members are looking for an excuse to be absent. With good reason. Everyone needs to eat every day, but nobody has energy for a banquet every day. The same holds true for prayer. One wonders whether the huge drop-off of people who used to attend church services daily isn't connected to this. People attended daily services more when those services were short, routine, predictable, and gave them the freedom to be as present or absent (in terms of emotional investment) as their energy and heart allowed on that given day.

Today, unfortunately, we are misled by a number of misconceptions about prayer and liturgy. Too commonly, we accept the following set of axioms as wise: Creativity and variety are always good. Every prayer-celebration should be one of high energy. Longer is better than shorter. Either you should pray with feeling or you shouldn't pray at all. Ritual is meaningless unless we are emotionally invested in it.

Each of these axioms is overly romantic, ill thought out, anthropologically naïve, and not helpful in sustaining a life of prayer. Prayer is a relationship, a long-term one, and lives by those rules. Relating to anyone long-term has its ups and downs. Nobody can be interesting all the time, sustain high energy all the time, or fully invest himself or herself all the time. Never travel with anyone who expects you to be interesting, lively, and emotionally invested all the time. Real life doesn't work that way. Neither does prayer. What sustains a relationship over the long term is ritual, routine, a regular rhythm that incarnates the commitment.

Imagine you have an aged mother in a nursing home and you've committed yourself to visiting her twice a week. How do you sustain yourself in this? Not by feeling, energy, or emotion, but by commitment, routine, and ritual. You go to visit her at a given time, not because you feel like it, but because it's time. You go to visit her in spite of the fact that you sometimes don't feel like it, that you sometimes can't give her the best of your heart, and that often you are tired, distracted, restless, overburdened, and occasionally sneaking a glance at your watch and wondering how soon you can make a graceful exit. Moreover, your conversation with her will not always be deep or about meaningful things. Occasionally there will be emotional satisfaction and the sense that something important was shared, but many times, perhaps most times, there will only be the sense that it was good that you were there and that an important life-giving connection has been nurtured and sustained, despite what seemingly occurred at the surface. You've been with your mother, and that's more important than whatever feelings or conversation might have taken place on a given day.

Prayer works the same way. That's why the saints and the great spiritual writers have always said that there is only one, nonnegotiable, rule for prayer: "Show up! Show up regularly!" The ups and downs of our minds and hearts are of secondary importance.

14

The EUCHARIST *as a* VIGIL, *as a* COMMUNAL RITE *of* WAITING

In her novel *The Underpainter*, Jane Urquhart describes a particularly painful time within the life of a woman named Sara. Sara's life is at a crossroads. A long-standing relationship has soured, she is unable to draw energy from much of what once gave her meaning, and she senses that she must move on, but is unsure of where to go and what to do. She needs something new to happen to her, some new person or event to appear and redefine her life. But what? Who? She doesn't know. She only knows, and very dimly, that she is waiting, keeping vigil somehow. Here is Urquhart's poignant description:

> Sometime during August of 1935, the last month of the last summer I spent at Silver Islet, Sara told me what it was like to wait.... She told me that over the period of the last winter she had finally realized that everything that she did or said—every activity—was either a variant of, or a substitute for, waiting and therefore had no relevance on its own.[13]

So, too, within each of our lives. We are always waiting. The Eucharist is meant to help us with that. Among other things, it is meant to be a vigil, a coming together to wait for someone or something new to happen to us. We meet in Eucharist to wait with each other. The Eucharist is meant to be a vigil. As Gerhard Lohfink puts it:

> The early apostolic communities cannot be understood outside of the matrix of intense expectation. They were communities awaiting Christ's return. They gathered in Eucharist for, among other reasons, to foster and sustain this awareness, namely, that they were living in wait, waiting for Christ's return.[14]

But what does that mean exactly? How is the Eucharist a vigil, a gathering together to wait? How, indeed, does any vigil work?

We keep vigil whenever we live our lives in the face of the fact that we are, consciously or unconsciously, waiting for someone or something new to come into our lives and give us a completeness that we are now missing. For example, we speak of a funeral vigil: a loved one has died. So we come together, usually in a chapel, to remember and celebrate the person who has died, but also to console one another as we wait for the sting of death to pass so the joy of life can return.

As mentioned, the sense of vigil can be conscious or unconscious. For example, when we sit at an airport or train station, waiting for a loved one to arrive, we are quite conscious that we are keeping vigil, waiting. Often, though, as in Urqu-

hart's description of Sara's waiting, we have only an inchoate sense of keeping vigil. We are, it would seem, doing other
things, but, underneath, we are keeping vigil. For example,
picture this:

Three women, each single and in her late thirties, meet
every Friday night to digest their week, let off some steam,
and enjoy each other's friendship. What they do varies: some
nights they share a bottle of wine and reminisce about old
college days as they watch a video, other nights they go to a
movie, and sometimes they simply go from work to a pub and
make an evening of it. They do different things, but they meet
weekly, ritually. What is happening here? A number of things:

At one level, they are simply celebrating friendship, pure
and simple. At another level, though, like Jane Urquhart's
Sara, they are keeping vigil. They are helping to sustain each
other as each of them, single and approaching midlife, is waiting for something or someone new to come into her life to
help redefine and reshape its next chapter. They aren't nec-
essarily looking for husbands or kids, though a powerful
imperative within their DNA no doubt pushes them in that
direction, but they are waiting. However dim that awareness,
they know that a chapter of their lives is winding down, that
things cannot stay as they are, that something or someone
new must enter and help them redefine their meaning. Their
coming together is partly to sustain each other as they wait
for this new something to appear.

What is true for these women is ultimately true for every
one of us. At the end of the day we are all, each in his or her
own way, single, inconsummate, waiting. None of us has the

complete symphony. Ninety-nine percent of the time we are waiting, longing for something new to appear in our lives.

The Eucharist is a vigil, a ritual, that brings us together, like those thirty-something singles, so that we can console and sustain each other within the mutual inconsummation of our lives. In the Eucharist we assure one another that we still have one another, that we still have God, and that we still have Christ's promise to, one day, wipe away our every ache and give us the ecstasy we so painfully crave. In the Eucharist we wait for Christ's return. We have sustained this ritual for two thousand years.

15

The EUCHARIST *as the* PRIESTLY PRAYER *of* CHRIST

Prayer is classically defined as *lifting mind and heart to God*. That's a good definition, but it needs an important qualification.

There are two essential kinds of prayer: Something we call *liturgical* prayer, the public prayer of the church, and something we call *private* or *devotional* prayer. Unfortunately we often confuse the two.

For example, although five hundred people might be sitting in meditation together in a church or praying the rosary together at a shrine, this is still private or devotional prayer. Conversely, someone might be praying the Office of the Church alone at home in an armchair, or a priest might be celebrating the Eucharist alone at a kitchen table, and this is public, liturgical prayer. The distinction, as we see from these examples, is not dependent upon the number of people participating, or whether the prayer is taking place in a church, or even whether the prayer is being prayed in a group or privately. The distinction is based upon something else. What?

Perhaps a change of names might help us understand the distinction: liturgical, public prayer might more aptly be called *priestly* prayer, while private and devotional prayer might better be termed *affective* prayer.

What is priestly prayer? It is the prayer *of* Christ *through* the church *for* the world. Our Christian belief is that Christ is still gathering us together around his word and is still offering an eternal act of love for the world. As an extension of that, we believe that whenever we meet together, in a church or elsewhere, to gather around the scriptures or to celebrate the Eucharist, we are entering into that prayer and sacrifice of Christ. This is liturgical prayer; it's Christ's prayer, not ours. We pray liturgically whenever we gather to celebrate the scriptures or the sacraments, or when we pray, in community or privately, something that is called the Prayer of the Church or the Office of the Church (Lauds and Vespers).

And this kind of prayer is not restricted to the ordained clergy. We are all priests by virtue of our baptism, and part of the implicit covenant we make with the community at our baptism is the commitment, when we reach adulthood, to pray habitually for the world through the liturgical Prayer of the Church.

What needs also to be highlighted here, since we easily miss this aspect, is that the church's liturgical prayer is for the world, not for itself. The church, in this world, does not exist for its own sake, but as an instrument of salvation for the world. Its function is to save the world, not itself. In liturgical prayer we pray with Christ, through the church, but for the world.

Affective prayer has a different intent. Though it has many forms—meditation, centering prayer, praying the rosary, devotional prayers of all kinds—it has a single aim, to draw us and our loved ones into deeper intimacy with Christ. In the end, no matter its particular form, all nonliturgical prayer ultimately aims at personal intimacy with God and is, ultimately too, private, even when it is done publicly or in a large group. All private and devotional prayer can be defined in this way: it is prayer that tries, in myriad ways, to open us or our loved ones up in such a way that we can hear God say to us, "I love you!"

It is important to know the following distinction when we go to pray: Which kind of prayer are we entering? To confuse the two is to risk doing both badly. For example, the person who feels frustrated because the liturgical ritual and interaction of a congregation inside a church service are felt as a hindrance and a distraction to the private devotional prayers she would like to be saying is confusing the two forms of prayer and is consequently doing both badly. The function of liturgical prayer is not first of all devotional.

Or sometimes the confusion leads someone to abandon one form of liturgical prayer altogether. I know a man who, after years of praying the Office of the Church, is substituting his own private prayer in its place because he doesn't find the ritual prayers personally meaningful. His private meditations now might well be wonderful affective prayer, but he is no longer praying the priestly prayer of Christ when he is praying in this way. We see this sometimes, too, in well-intentioned, but badly planned, church services where what is intended to

be a liturgical service ends up being a guided private meditation. However well done and powerful, such a service neither
uses scripture nor prays for the world.

Churches themselves struggle with this. Roman Catholics,
Anglicans, Episcopalians, and mainline Protestant churches
have a strong liturgical tradition, sometimes to the detriment
of affective prayer. Evangelical and Pentecostal churches, on
the other hand, have a strong focus on affective prayer, sometimes to the point of neglecting liturgical prayer almost entirely.

We would probably all do ourselves a favor by having two
prayer shawls, each embroidered separately, *Priestly Prayer* and
Affective Prayer.

One of the things asked of us by adulthood itself, and
more especially by our baptism, is that we pray for others.
Like the high priests of old, we need to offer up prayers daily
for the whole world. Indeed we are all priests, ordained by
the sacred oils of baptism and consecrated by the archetypal
burdens that have given us wrinkles and gray hair. As adults,
elders, we have both the privilege and the responsibility to,
as scripture puts it, "make prayer and entreaty, aloud and in
silent tears, for ourselves and for the people." All of us, lay and
cleric alike, need to offer up priestly prayer each day.

But how do we do that? How do we pray priestly prayers?
We pray as priests, as Jesus prayed in the seventeenth chapter of John's Gospel, every time we sacrifice self-interest for
the good of the community. That's priestly prayer in its wid-
est sense. However, we pray that prayer, formally and sacra-
mentally, whenever we pray the Prayer of the Church, namely,

the Eucharist or the Divine Office. This kind of prayer, called liturgy, is what keeps incarnate the priestly prayer of Christ.

In priestly prayer, we pray not just for ourselves, nor ideally by ourselves, but we pray as a microcosm of the whole world, even as we pray for the whole world. In this kind of prayer we lift up our voices to God, not as a private offering, but in such a way as to give a voice to the Earth itself. In essence, when we pray at the Eucharist or at the Divine Office, we are saying this:

Lord, God, I stand before you as a microcosm of the Earth itself, to give it voice: See in my openness the world's openness; in my infidelity the world's infidelity; in my sincerity the world's sincerity; in my hypocrisy the world's hypocrisy; in my generosity the world's generosity; in my selfishness the world's selfishness; in my attentiveness the world's attentiveness; in my distraction the world's distraction; in my desire to praise you the world's desire to praise you; and in my self-preoccupation, the world's forgetfulness of you. For I am of the Earth, a piece of Earth, and the Earth opens or closes to you through my body, my soul, and my voice. I am your priest on earth.

And what I hold up for you today is all that is in this world, both of joy and of suffering. I offer you the bread of the world's achievements, even as I offer you the wine of its failure, the blood of all that's crushed as those achievements take place. I offer you the powerful of our world, our rich, our famous, our athletes, our artists, our movie stars, our entrepreneurs, our young, our healthy, and everything that's creative and bursting with life, even as I offer you those who are weak, feeble, aged, crushed, sick, dying, and victimized. I offer to you all the pagan beauties, pleasures, and joys of this life, even as I stand with you under the cross, affirming that the one who is excluded from earthly pleasure is the cornerstone of the community. I offer you the strong and arrogant, along with the weak and gentle of heart, asking you to bless both and to stretch my heart so that it can, like you, hold and bless everything that is. I offer you both the wonders and the pains of this world, your world.

To pray like this is to pray liturgically, as priest. And we pray like this each time we go to the Eucharist or when we, with others or alone, pray the Divine Office of the church. It is particularly this latter prayer, the Divine Office (also called Breviary or Liturgy of the Hours), that is available daily as the priestly prayer for those of us who are not ordained ministers in the church. And this is especially true for two of those liturgical Hours, Lauds (Morning Prayer) and Vespers (Evening Prayer). They, unlike the other Hours, which are more the particular domain of monks and professional contemplatives, are the ordinary priestly prayer of the laity.

And what is important in praying them is to remember that these are not prayers that we say for ourselves, nor indeed prayers whose formulae we need to find meaningful or relevant. Unlike private prayer and contemplation, where we should change methods whenever praying becomes too dry or sterile, Lauds and Vespers are prayers of the universal church that are in essence intended to be communal and priestly. They don't have to be relevant for our private lives. We pray them as elders, as baptized adults, as priests, to invoke God's blessing upon the world.

And whenever we do pray them, we are, in microcosm, the voice, body, and soul of the Earth itself, continuing the high priesthood of Christ, as we offer prayers and entreaties, aloud and in silent tears, to a God who can save us.

PART THREE

A SPIRITUALITY *of* *the* EUCHARIST:

Receive, Give Thanks, Break, Share

The Eucharist is not intended to be simply a ritual prayer within which we participate regularly, but is also meant to be something that touches and colors every area of our lives. Scripture exhorts us to "pray always." Obviously this does not mean that we should always be saying prayers. We would have to stop living normal lives. It refers to something deeper. The challenge is to try to live our lives in such a way that our whole life, in a manner of speaking, becomes a prayer.

It is the same with the Eucharist. We need to be living and breathing Eucharist all the time, not just at those times when we are in church. The Eucharist needs to be a defining attitude, a way we meet life, receive it, and share it with others. It needs to be a spirituality, namely, a way we undergo the presence of God and others in this world.

A spirituality of the Eucharist might be defined in the four Eucharistic phrases that Jesus gave us: *receive, give thanks, break, share*. These simple words contain both a full Christology and a full spirituality. They define Christ and they tell how we should live as his disciples.

Receive

Some years ago I sat in on a series of lectures on the theology of the Trinity given by James Mackey. At one point he shared this story:

A man he knew was once a member of a hunting expedition in Africa. One morning this man left the camp early, by himself, and hiked several miles into the jungle, where he surprised and eventually bagged two wild turkeys. Buckling his catch to his belt, he headed back toward camp. At some point, however, he sensed that he was being followed. With his senses heightened by fear, he stopped, hands on his rifle, and looked around. His fears were dispelled when he saw what was happening. Following him at a distance was a naked and obviously starved adolescent boy. The boy's objective was food, not threat. Seeing this, the man stopped, unbuckled his belt, and, letting the turkeys fall to the ground, backed off and gestured to the boy that he could come and take the birds. The boy ran up to the two birds, but, inexplicably, refused to pick them up. He was, seemingly, still asking for something else. Perplexed, the man tried both by words and by gestures to indicate to the boy that he could have the birds. Still the boy refused to pick them up. Finally, in desperation, unable to explain what he still wanted, the boy backed off several meters from the dead birds and stood with outstretched and open hands . . . waiting, *waiting until the man came and placed the birds in his hands.* He had, despite hunger, fear, and intense need, refused to *take* the birds. He waited until they were *given* to him; he received them.

That simple story is a mini-course in moral theology. It summarizes all of Christ's moral teachings and the entire Ten Commandments. If we, like this boy, would always wait until life was given to us as gift, as opposed to taking it as if by right, seizing it, or raping it, we would never break a single Commandment. Moreover, we would have in our lives the first and most important virtue of all, the sense that all is gift, that nothing is owed us by right.

In a way, this story is the opposite of the original sin story. In the Adam and Eve story, God *gives* them life and then adds a commandment which, on the surface, appears strange and arbitrary: "Do not eat of the fruit of the tree of knowledge of good and evil." What is this commandment?

In essence, what God is telling Adam and Eve is this: "I am going to *give* you life. You may *receive* that life, but you may never *take* it. To take it is to ruin and destroy the gift that it is." Adam and Eve's sin was, ultimately, one of rape, the act of robbing, despoiling, and taking by force something that can only be had when it is received gratefully and respectfully as gift. Their sin, as is all sin, was an act of irreverence, the failure to respect the deepest foundations of a reality that is love-contoured.

Simply put, the original sin was a failure in gratitude and receptivity, the failure to respect a gift. It is no accident that the author of the story employs images (nakedness, shame) that are suggestive of sexual violation. That is the very point of this story, except that the rape being talked about here is wider than sex. In turning away from the posture of receptivity to the posture of seizing, Adam and Eve began to take by force, as by right, what was theirs only as gift. The result of that is always shame, a darkened mind, rationalization, and the beginnings of a dysfunctional world.

In the story of the boy who refused to take the very food he needed to live on, we see what the opposite of original sin looks like. That kind of patient, receptive waiting and respect might aptly be termed "original virtue"—and it is needed today. In a world whose spirit too easily defines morality by achievement and the accumulation of things, that invites us to demand our rights, and suggests that "God helps those who help themselves," it is radically countercultural to suggest that a patient waiting to be given life (even when we are hungry) is better than the active seizing of it. To Adam and Eve, God said, "It is good, but it is gift, respect it as such. Don't ever *take* the apple!" All of morality can be summarized in that line.

Allow me a further example:

Several years ago a young Benedictine monk shared the following story with me. He lived in a monastery that kept a fairly strict rule. Their observance of poverty and obedience required that he ask permission of his abbot before purchasing anything, even the smallest object. If he wanted to buy a new shirt, he needed the abbot's permission. Likewise if he wanted to take some stationery supplies from the storeroom, a pen or some paper, he needed permission. For years, he felt that this was belittling. "I felt like a child," he said. "It seemed silly to me that a grown man should have to ask permission to buy a new shirt! I looked at men my own age who were married, raising children, paying for houses, and presidents of companies, and I felt that our rule reduced me to a child and I resented it."

But eventually his attitude changed: "I came to realize that there is an important spiritual and psychological principle in our rule, in having to ask permission to buy or use something. Ultimately none of us owns anything, and nothing comes to us by right. Everything is a gift, including life itself, everything should have to be asked for and nothing should be taken as if it was ours by right. We should be grateful to God just for giving us a little space. Now when I ask permission from the abbot, I no longer feel like a child. Rather I feel that I am more properly in tune with the way things should be in a gift-oriented universe where nobody has a right to ultimately claim anything as his own. Everyone should have to ask for permission before buying or using anything."

His story reminded me of an incident in my own life: When I was a novice in our Oblate novitiate, our novice-master tried to impress upon us the meaning of religious poverty by making us write two Latin words, *Ad Usum,* inside of every book that was given us for our own use. Literally the words translate "for use." The idea was that although a book was given to you for your personal use, you were never to think that you actually owned it. Real ownership lay elsewhere; you were only a steward of someone else's property. And this idea was then extended to everything else that you were given for your personal use—your clothes, your sports equipment, things you received from your family, and even your toiletries and toothbrush. You got to use them, but they were not really yours. You had them *ad usam*.

One of the young men in that novitiate eventually left our community and went on to become a medical doctor. He remains a close friend, and one day while I was in his office I picked up one of his medical textbooks. I opened the cover and there were the words: *Ad Usam*. When I asked him about this, he made a comment to this effect: "Even though I no longer belong to a religious order and no longer have the vow of poverty, I still like to live by the principle that our novice-master taught us: in the end, we don't really own anything. These books aren't really my own, even though I've paid for them. They're mine to use, temporarily. Nothing really belongs to anybody, and I try not to forget that."

Both of these stories can help remind us of something that deep down we already know but tend to forget: that what ultimately undergirds all spirituality, all morality, and all authentic human relationship is the unalterable truth that everything comes to us as gift, so that nothing can ever be owned as ours by right. Life is a gift, breath is a gift, our body is a gift, food is a gift, any love given us is a gift, friendship is a gift, our talents are a gift, our toothbrush is a gift, and the shirts, pencils, pens, and medical textbooks we use are each of them a gift. We get to have them, *ad usam*, but we should never nurse the illusion that we own them, that they are ours, that we can claim them by right. Metaphorically there should be an abbot in each of our lives from whom we should ask for permission to buy or use anything. That would be a recipe for health.

In those moments when we are most in touch with ourselves (and generally those are the moments when we most feel our vulnerability and contingency), we sense that truth. The reverse is also true, at moments when we feel strong, in control, and aware of our own power, we tend to forget this truth and cling to the illusion that things are ours by right. Maybe if we all had to ask permission to buy a new toothbrush or a new item of clothing we would be more aware that everything we think we own is really only ours *ad usam*.

A spirituality of the Eucharist invites us to have this kind of attitude of receptivity toward all of life: *Receive*. This word, which describes our posture in approaching the Eucharist, is also meant to mandate an entire way of living, wherein we are asked to acknowledge always, by the very way we receive everything, that everything is gift, and that nothing comes to us as owed.

Give Thanks

A Jewish folk tale tells of a young man who aspired to great holiness. After some time at working to achieve it, he went to see his rabbi. "Rabbi," he announced, "I think I have achieved sanctity." "Why do you think that?" asked the rabbi. "Well," responded the young man, "I've been practicing virtue and discipline for some time now, and I have grown quite proficient at them. From the time the sun rises until it sets, I practice a rigorous asceticism: I take no food or water. All day long, I do all kinds of hard work for others and I never expect to be thanked. If I have temptations of the flesh, I roll in the snow or in thorn bushes until they go away, and then at night, before bed, I practice the ancient monastic discipline and administer lashes to my bare back. I have strongly disciplined myself so as to become holy."

The rabbi was silent for a time. Then he took the young man by the arm and led him to a window and pointed to an old horse that was just being led away by its master. "I have been observing that horse for some time," the rabbi said, "and I've noticed that it doesn't get fed or watered from morning to night. All day long it has to do work for people, and it never gets thanked. I often see it rolling around in snow or in bushes, as horses are prone to do, and frequently I see it get whipped, but that, young man, is a horse, not a saint!"

This is an insightful parable because it shows how simplistic it is to identify sanctity and virtue with self-renunciation and the capacity to do what is difficult. In popular thought there is often an oversimplified spiritual equation: saint = horse; what is more difficult is always better. But that can be wrong.

To be a saint is to be motivated by gratitude, nothing more and nothing less. Scripture, everywhere and always, makes this point. For example, the sin of Adam and Eve, as we saw, was first and foremost a failure in receptivity and gratitude. God gives them life, each other, and the garden, and asks them only to receive it properly, in gratitude—and then give thanks. The original sin was precisely Adam and Eve's refusal to do this. Instead they *took* the apple, taking as though by right what could only be received gratefully as gift. It is no coincidence that when giving us the Eucharist, Christ said, "Receive and give thanks." Only after doing this do we go on to "break and share." Before all else, we must first give thanks.

To give thanks, to be properly grateful, is the most primary of all religious attitudes. Proper gratitude is the ultimate virtue. It defines sanctity. Saints, holy persons, are people who are grateful, people who see and receive everything as gift. The converse is also true. Anyone who takes life and love for granted should not ever be confused with a saint.

When I was a seminarian, I once spent a week in a hospital, on a public ward, with a knee injury. One night a patient was brought into our ward from the emergency room. His pain was so severe that his groans kept us awake. The doctors had just worked on him, and it was then left to a single nurse to attend to him. Several times that night she entered the room to minister to him—changing bandages, giving medication, and so on. Each time, as she walked away from his bed, he would, despite the extreme pain, thank her. Finally, after a number of these occurrences, she said to him, "Sir, you don't need to thank me. This is my job!" "Ma'am," he replied, "it's nobody's job to take care of me! Nobody owes me that. I want to thank you!"

I was struck by that: how, even in his great pain, this man remained conscious of the fact that life, love, care, and everything else come to us as gift, not as owed. He genuinely appreciated what this nurse was doing for him, and he was right: It isn't anybody's job to take care of us! It is our propensity to forget this that gets us into trouble. The failure to be properly grateful, and to take as owed what is offered as a gift, lies at the root of many of our deepest resentments toward others and their resentments toward us. Invariably when we get angry at someone, especially at those closest to us, it is precisely because we feel that we are not being appreciated (that is, thanked) properly. Conversely, I suspect, more than a few people harbor resentments toward us because we, consciously or unconsciously, think that it is their job to take care of us. Like Adam and Eve, we take their gift as if it is ours by right, instead of recognizing and acknowledging that it is gift. This goes against the very contours of love, the original sin. The Eucharist invites us in the opposite direction. Everything we receive in life is gift and must be received as gift.

Moreover, one of the ways that we thank the giver of a gift is by thoroughly enjoying the gift. Proper enjoyment is a Eucharistic virtue.

Several years ago, one of my sisters died of cancer. She was an Ursuline nun who possessed a deep faith, and had for many years given herself over to the service of others with an unselfishness that was exceptional. Yet, despite all this, she found it very hard to die, to let go. Why? I have seen others, with less faith, let go much more easily.

In my sister's case the difficulty was not that she was afraid of God, or the afterlife, or the unknown. She didn't have these fears. The reason she found it hard to die was simply that she loved her life so deeply. She thoroughly enjoyed her life. She basked in her friendships, in her work, in her family, in good food, in good weather, in good chocolate (her weakness). She was not a particularly reflective person, but she was not a moody one, either. Instead she was impatient with those who gave life too much of a tragic or stoic twist. This she considered pompous, false, a waste. Life, for her, was good, something to be drunk in with delight. In her view, you were meant to enjoy life, even if you ended up with a double chin. For her, this was what separated the Christian from the stoic. The formula worked for her. She had a happy life, did eventually develop a double chin, and died a deeply loved woman.

What this story highlights is something that is too often not sufficiently emphasized within spirituality: that the highest compliment someone can give to a gift-giver is to thoroughly enjoy the gift. The highest compliment we can give to God, our Creator, is to truly enjoy the gift of life. The best way to pay for a beautiful moment is to enjoy it.

More often than not, this is not the message that has come

through in Christian spirituality, or in virtually every other spirituality and secular philosophy for that matter. Mostly what has been presented as mature, as the ideal to be imitated, is the ideal of the stoic, the Hamlet figure, the person who is somehow above and detached from the enjoyments, pleasures, and delights of the ordinary person. A saint who craves chocolate? There aren't many icons, outside of Buddhism, that depict saintly figures with a double chin. We are the poorer for that. We have mistaken Hamlet for Jesus, stoicism for Christianity, depression for detachment.

A spirituality of the Eucharist, as inviting us to gratitude, can serve a corrective here. The Eucharistic person is not the noble antihero who luxuriates in despair, but the child of the kingdom, the grace-merry person who, while sharing fully in the tears of this world, is ultimately distinguished through his or her laughter. To consider life as tragic is to not live out the Eucharist. It is also to not imitate Christ, who shocked as many people with his capacity to enjoy this Earth as he did with his challenge to live in the face of the fact that this Earth is not our true home.

Paradoxically, it is invariably those who accept most clearly that this world is not our true home who also have the ability to enjoy life most fully. Occasionally, too, they have double chins. My sister did, and not just because she enjoyed chocolate. She lived out the Eucharist, part of which is an invitation to thank every gift-giver by thoroughly enjoying the gift.

Give thanks! These words are not just a mandate for the moral posture we should have when receiving the Eucharist.

They also invite us to stand before all of life in a certain posture of gratefulness, realizing always that it is nobody's job to love and take care of us, and that love and care come to us as gifts that need to be be acknowledged. Indeed the very word *Eucharist* means gratitude.

Break

A parable about a peasant runs along these lines:

There once lived a peasant in Crete who deeply loved his life. He enjoyed tilling the soil, feeling the warm sun on his naked back as he worked the fields, and feeling the soil under his feet. He loved the planting, the harvesting, and the very smell of nature. He loved his wife and his family and his friends, and he enjoyed being with them, eating together, drinking wine, talking, and making love. And especially he loved Crete, his beautiful island! The earth, the sky, the sea—they were his! This was his home.

One day he sensed death approaching. What he feared was not what lay beyond, for he knew God's goodness and had lived a good life. No, he feared leaving Crete, his wife, his children, his friends, his home, and his land. And so, as he prepared to die, he grasped in his right hand a few grains of soil from his beloved Crete and told his loved ones to bury him with it.

He died, awoke, and found himself at heaven's gate, the soil still in his hands and heaven's gate firmly barred against him. Eventually Saint Peter emerged through the gates and spoke to him: "You've lived a good life, and we've a place for you inside, but you cannot enter unless you drop that handful of soil. You cannot enter as you are now!"

Reluctant to drop the soil, the man protested, "Why? Why must I let go of this soil? Indeed, I cannot! Whatever is inside those gates, I have no knowledge of. But this soil, I know. It's my life, my work, my wife and children, it's what I know and love, it's Crete! Why should I let it go for something I know nothing about?"

Peter answered, "When you get to heaven you will know why. It's too difficult to explain. I am asking you to trust, trust that God can give you something better than a few grains of soil."

But the man refused. In the end, silent and seemingly defeated, Peter left him, closing the large gates behind. Several minutes later the gates opened a second time and this time, a young child emerged. She did not try to coax the man into letting go of the soil in his hand. She simply took his hand and, as she did, it opened and the soil of Crete spilled to the ground. She then led him through the gates.

A shock awaited him as he entered heaven. There, before him, lay all of Crete!

Parable and story can touch affective levels in us and move us in rationally inexplicable ways, and so a story of this kind should not be given too much explanation. It should be more an object for meditation than explanation. Nonetheless, a tiny application might be helpful.

Break! How do we break so as to live the Eucharist within our daily lives? When Jesus links the idea of breaking to the Eucharist, the rending and breaking down that he is talking about have to do with narcissism, individualism, pride, self-serving ambition, and all the other things that prevent us from letting go of those things inside of us that prevent us from giving ourselves to others. Buddhist spirituality suggests that most everything that is wrong in the world can be explained in one image, that of the group photo. Whenever anyone looks at a group photo, the person invariably looks first at how he or she turned out and only afterwards considers whether or not it is a good picture of the group. Breaking the Eucharistic bread invites us to look first at how the group turned out.

It invites us, too, into a deeper understanding of what it means to be together at a Eucharist: our Eucharists, like our homes and places of work, bring us together even as we are still filled with distrust, jealousy, paranoia, and misunderstandings. We stand around the Eucharistic table with the same wounds we bring to our other tables.

Eucharist, then, is meant not just to celebrate our joys and gratitude, but also to break us open, to make us groan in anguish, to lay bare our mistrust, to lessen our jealousies and break down the distances that separate us. What the Eucharist asks of us is vulnerability, humility, contrition, and forgiveness. Bitterness, hatred, and suspicion are meant to disappear at a Eucharist.

But it is on this very point that, perhaps, we struggle the most at Eucharist. What's wrong at the Eucharist generally is not that we don't pray and sing, but that we don't break down. There is too little anguish in our Eucharists. To become one in heart with each other involves precisely breaking down, anguish, the painful letting go of distrust, selfishness, bitterness, hurt, jealousy, and even of shyness. All these things keep us apart and all of these are strongly held and fiercely guarded inside of ourselves. If our Eucharists do not succeed in breaking down the barriers that separate us from each other, then we have little reason to hope that these barriers will break down in our world. If we cannot succeed at forming community in church, we will not succeed in forming it elsewhere.

Jesus was effective in leading us into community because he was vulnerable. He was often in anguish, not least at the Last Supper itself. It is interesting to reflect upon what Jesus must have been feeling when he instituted the Eucharist. What were his feelings at the Last Supper? Joy and thanksgiving and love for those at table with him, surely. But beyond this, his heart must have felt deep anguish and fear at the prospect of the humiliation and pain that was now a certainty before intimacy and community would be achieved, At the Last Supper, Jesus surely would have felt broken, poured out, empty, heartbroken, frightened, and vulnerable. Shouldn't we be feeling the same things sometimes at the Eucharist?

It would perhaps do us all good occasionally to leave the Eucharist and, instead of heading off for a lively brunch with family and friends, go off, as Jesus did after the first Eucharist, to a lonely place to agonize and sweat blood over love and separation and to ask God to give us the strength to drink from the chalice of vulnerability.

At the Eucharist we are meant to break down. Livelier liturgies and better homilies alone will not resolve the common complaint that our church services are not meaningful enough. That complaint has a far deeper prong: our church services aren't meaningful enough because, most times, the bread and wine are the only things that change. *We* don't change! Our hearts remain just as suspicious, jealous, fearful, and hard as they were before. That doesn't make for very meaningful liturgy.

Among other reasons, we go to the Eucharist to break down, to try, through our communion with God and others, to crack open the casings of our selfishness, to break out of our self-centered dreams, and to open our hands and let go of some of the things to which we are clinging too tightly. This is symbolized by the ritual before communion when the Eucharistic bread is broken. It is broken so that it can be distributed, but it is broken, too, to symbolize a way of life, a spirituality. The Eucharist invites us to imitate Christ's sacrifice, his letting himself be broken and emptied out of love.

Saint Augustine, in his Eucharistic sermons, was fond of telling people, "If you receive this well, you are what you receive . . . for the loaf that contains Christ is made up of many individual kernels of grain, but these kernels must, to become the loaf containing Christ, first be ground up and then baked together by fire."[15]

Share

As a young seminarian I spent a summer working in a retreat house. The priest directing the house had a curious hobby: he polished stones. During long, solitary walks he would watch for small stones that looked interesting, and when he found one that looked as if it might have value, he would bring it back to his workshop. There he had a small barrel-drum that was itself filled with small, very hard stones. He would take the stone he had found, his potential gem, and place it inside the barrel-drum, add some water, seal the drum tightly, and turn on an electric motor that would slowly rotate the drum. After several weeks of this, he would open the drum and search for his little stone. Many times he would find that it had simply disappeared, the weeks of grinding having reduced it to gravel and sand. If the stone, however, had value, he would find it now, polished, gleaming, a gem with all its rough edges rubbed off and all useless gravel and sand knocked out of it.

There is something in that image about our lives in family and community. There used to be an expression in popular spiritual literature: *Families and communities are schools of charity.* I remember reading it as a novice many years ago, and very naïvely and very badly misunderstanding it. My simple thought then was, *Yes, that makes sense! When you live within a family or some other community, it gives you a lot of chances to practice patience, forgiveness, and understanding—as you deal with other people's faults!* How wrong I was! What that expression suggests is not, first of all, that we grow in charity and maturity by putting up patiently with other people's faults, but that real relationship, actual interaction within family and community, deflates our fantasies, makes us see reality, punctures our self-centeredness, and against every protest, denial, and rationalization we can muster, shows us how selfish and immature we often are.

We cannot live very long within any community—marriage, family, religious community, or genuine friendship—without becoming aware of our faults and narrowness. We either begin to grow up, or we leave. Sadly, today the temptation is most often to leave. The misguided theory is that we grow mature by growing away, especially away from the family and community within which, by circumstance, we find ourselves. The idea is that we will be happy—and available for real family and friendship—if we are free spirits, soaring, unattached, unencumbered.

I remember a young nun to whom I once served as spiritual director. Before entering the convent, she had lived alone in her own apartment and was quite popular. She had many friends and was, to her own mind, quite a mature, giving, and unselfish person. Not long after joining a religious community, where she lived in close quarters with other novices and those directing the novitiate, she began to experience major problems with her relationships. She was often at odds with her peers and her directors, who, tactfully and otherwise, told her that she was somewhat self-centered and immature. She was particularly frustrated because often the tensions arose over very petty things.

"It must be the community that's causing this," she told me

during one of our sessions. "I was never a petty, selfish person when I lived alone!" Then, when I asked why she continued to stay in the convent if that was the case, she replied: "Because, in my better moments, I know that if I ran off now and got married, probably most of the things that are happening here would begin to happen again! Some of this stuff would catch up with me again. When I lived alone it was lonely, but it was easier. You didn't have to live your life under a microscope. But you could easily fool yourself, too!"

What was happening to her in that community? The stone was being polished! She was being churned in the barrel-drum that is called family, community. The other stones were knocking some rough edges off of her and rubbing her free of considerable useless gravel and sand. It was painful and humiliating for her, but she was learning the most valuable lesson of all, how to share your life in reality as opposed to fantasy. She was in a school of charity. She was being purified.

Family and community aren't boring; they're terrifying. They're too full of searing revelations; there we have no place to hide. In family life, our selfishness and immaturities are reflected back to us through eyes that are steady and unblinking. Staying within them is often the hell that leads to heaven.

Share! The Eucharist, as a spirituality, invites us into community and family. To live out the Eucharist in daily life is to share our everyday lives with each other.

Some years ago I participated in a workshop on Zen prayer. The woman leading the sessions, a longtime devotee of Zen who sat in private meditation for several hours each day, was describing some of the spiritual insights she experienced during those prayer sessions. At one point I asked her, "When you are sitting for those long periods in private prayer, how would you compare what you experience there with what you experience at your family table?" Her answer: "There is really no comparison! During my prayer times I touch transcendence. Mealtimes with family or friends are nice, but they aren't prayer."

I said nothing in response then, but I'm Christian enough to not be comfortable with her answer. Scripture tells us: "God is love, and whoever abides in love, abides in God, and God in him or her."[16] As it is referred to in this passage, love does not refer in any particular way to romantic love. The text is not saying, "Those who fall in love, abide in God," though that may often be true, too. The passage might well be translated in this way: "God is shared existence, and those who break open their lives and gratefully share them with others already live inside of God."

Theologians tell us that God is as much a verb as a noun. God is a trinity of persons: Father, Son, and Holy Spirit. For Christians this is more than a simple dogma that we are asked to accept, even if we don't understand it. It is something that invites us to a whole way of life: God is a family, a community of persons sharing life together in such a way that a spirit, an energy of gratitude and joy, flows out of that shared life. We are asked to do the same—to share our lives with one another in such a way that joy and gratitude flow out as an energy that nurtures others. Life in the spirit is, quite simply, life shared with others.

Sometimes when I preach on the trinity, I make a suggestion to people: If you want to try to understand the trinity, don't isolate yourself with triangles or shamrocks and try to figure out how three can be one and one can be three. Instead, sit down at table with family or friends, let the food, wine, and conversation flow, and simply *experience* the trinity. God is found not just in the silent innermost depths of our hearts; God is found, too, in the experience of sharing life.

Jean-Paul Sartre once suggested that community is hell. On a given day, the tensions inherent within community life can certainly make that seem true. However, in our better moments, we all know that the reverse is the truth: alienation and aloneness are hell; shared life is heaven.

The Eucharist is an invitation to us not just to come together in church to celebrate a sacred ritual that Jesus left us. The Eucharist invites us to commit ourselves, inside our families and communities, to share all aspects of our lives with others.

PART FOUR

OUR ONE GREAT FIDELITY

In one of his sermons on the Eucharist, Ronald Knox[17] made this observation: Throughout two thousand years of history, Christians, both whole churches and individual believers, have consistently been able to ignore many of Jesus' key commandments and invitations. We have either been too weak to follow his counsels or we have rationalized them away in some way.

And so, to a large extent, we have exempted ourselves from the demands to love our enemies; to turn the other cheek when attacked; to forgive seventy times seven; to leave our gift at the altar and first go and seek reconciliation with our brother before we worship; to place justice on the same level as worship; to see mercy as more important than dogma; to not commit adultery, not steal, not call someone a fool, not tell lies, not give in to jealousy. We have, in virtually every one of these areas, individually and collectively, a history of infidelity and rationalization.

But we have, for the most part, been faithful and consistent throughout all the years to one of Jesus' commands, to celebrate the Eucharist, to meet together in every circumstance and share his word and break bread and drink wine in his memory. The older I get, the more meaningful this bald fact becomes to me, both as it pertains to the church and as it applies to me personally. Whenever possible, I try to celebrate Eucharist every day, for many reasons. The Eucharist contains and carries many deep realities: it helps continue the incarnation of God in history; it is God's physical embrace; it is an intensification of our community together as Christians; it is the new manna that God gives to nurture his people; it is our family meal together as believers; it is Christ's sacrifice which we commemorate ritually; it is God's gift of reconciliation and forgiveness; it is an invitation to a deeper discipleship; it is a banquet table opened up for the poor; it is a vigil service within which we wait for Christ to return; and it is Christ's priestly prayer for the world.

But I go to Eucharist daily for another reason as well, a more personal one: this is the one place where I can be faithful, where I can essentially measure up. I can't always control how I feel or how I think, and I can't always measure up morally and spiritually, but inside of my perpetual inadequacy and occasional doubt and confusion, I can be faithful in this one deep way. I can go to the Eucharist regularly.

With age, I am growing less confident or sure about my knowledge of God, religion, and life. As knowledge deepens, it also widens and begins to take on softer edges. Unlike the more confident years of my youth, I now live with the sense that my understanding of God's ways is a long way from being adequate, let alone normative. The mystery we live in is huge, and the more we grasp the magnitude of the cosmic and spiritual world, the more we grasp, too, how ineffable is God. God truly is beyond us, beyond language, beyond imagination, and even beyond feeling. We can know God, but can never understand God. And so we must be more humble, both in our theology and in our ecclesiology. Mostly we don't know what we are doing. The Eucharist, because it is the one ritual given us by Jesus himself, is one of our places of confidence.

Moreover, the older I get, the more I see, too, how blind I am to my own hypocrisies and how weak and rationalizing is my human nature. I don't always know when I'm rationalizing or biased or following Christ properly. And, even when I do, I don't always have the strength or will to do what I know is right. And so I lean heavily on the invitation that Jesus left us on the night before he died, to break bread and drink wine in his memory and to trust that this, if all else is uncertain, is what I should be doing while I wait for him to return.

Sometimes, when he was instructing a couple for marriage, Dietrich Bonhoeffer, the great Lutheran priest and martyr, would caution them with words to this effect: Right now you are in love and you believe that your love can sustain your marriage. It can't. But your marriage can sustain your love!

The Eucharist is such a ritual-container for Christians. We can't sustain our faith, charity, forgiveness, and hope on the basis of feeling or thought, but we can sustain them through the Eucharist. We can't always be clear-headed or warm-hearted; we can't always be sure that we know the exact path of God; and we won't always measure up morally and humanly to what faith asks of us. But we can be faithful in this one deep way: we can go to the Eucharist regularly.

PART FIVE

THREE
FAMOUS SERMONS
on the EUCHARIST

Saint Augustine (AD 354–430) is perhaps the most influential and important theologian in Christian history. He is also one of the thinkers who most deeply influenced Western thought. In a manner of speaking, Augustine helped write the software, the commonsense conceptions, within which we think today in the Western world.

What follows are three of the homilies that he gave on the Eucharist.[18] Each of these was delivered at a Eucharist on Easter Sunday morning, and was intended for those who had been baptized the night before at the Easter vigil and were receiving communion for just the second time (having received it for the first time just hours before at the Easter vigil service). These persons, the newly baptized, would not yet ever have heard a sermon on the Eucharist, even though they had received communion the night before. This was because of a discipline practiced in the early church, called the *Disciplina Arcani*, wherein Christians were not allowed to speak publicly to the non-baptized about the Eucharist, nor were those who were not baptized ever allowed to see or participate in a Eucharist.

Why the secrecy? There were a variety of reasons. No doubt Christians then were influenced by the various mystery cults around them, and wanted to keep some mystique around their central rituals. But the deeper reason, as we saw earlier, had little to do with mystery religions or wanting to radiate a certain mystique about the Eucharist. It had to do with the Christian belief that the intimacy of the Eucharist, like all deep intimacy, especially sexual intimacy, needs proper propriety: you don't make love in public. Beyond being unhealthily exhibitionistic, it cheapens the mystery. Hence the Eucharist was shrouded with a certain secrecy, and even the catechumens who were preparing to enter the church through baptism were not given an explanation of it, nor were they allowed to see it or participate in it until they had been baptized.

This is a literal translation from the original Latin text. Good grammar will be sacrificed in function of trying to render the text more literally.

First Sermon: Sermon 227,
In Die Paschae *IV* (Ad Infantes,
de Sacramentis)

I am mindful of the promise that I made to you who are just baptized that in a sermon I would explain the sacrament of the Lord's table, the sacrament that you see also now at this moment and in which you became sharers last night. You ought to receive it daily. This bread that you see upon the altar, sanctified by the word of God, is the body of Christ. This cup, rather what the cup contains, sanctified by the word of God, is the blood of Christ. These things, bread and wine, are what the Lord Christ wanted to entrust to us. They are his body and blood that he shed for us for the forgiveness of sins. If you have received this well, you are what you have received.

For the Apostle Paul says: "Many as we are, we are one bread one body" (1 Corinthians 10:17). In this way the Apostle exposed the sacrament of the table of the Lord: "We are one loaf, one bread, many as we are." It is entrusted to you in this loaf how much you must love unity. For surely this loaf has not been made from one grain of corn, has it? But the grains of corn were separated before they came to be one loaf: they were joined together by water after having been ground up. For if the many kernels are not ground and are not moistened by water, then any single kernel would not come at all to this form, which we call a loaf. And in this way, you too were ground as it were [in your preparation for baptism] by the humiliation of fasting and by the sacrament of exorcism. After baptism by water you were sprinkled, so to speak, in order to acquire the form of a loaf. But still without fire, there is not yet a loaf of bread. But what does fire signify? It is a chrism. For the oil of our fire is the sacrament of the Holy Spirit.

Pay attention to the Acts of the Apostles when they are read. We are just now starting the reading of this book [in the liturgy]: Today we have began the book that is called the Acts of the Apostles. He who wishes to make progress has something to start from. When you come together in the church, put away empty talk and be attentive to Holy Scripture. We are your books. *Therefore, pay attention, and see that the Holy Spirit will come at Pentecost. And the Holy Spirit will come in this way: He manifests Himself in tongues of fire. For He breathes charity into us by which we ardently desire God and disdain the sinful world, and our chaff will be burned up, and our hearts purified like gold. Therefore the Holy Spirit comes, after water and fire: and thus you become a loaf of bread, which is the body of Christ.*

Keep the sacrament in this order. First, after a prayer you are admonished to lift up your hearts. This is becoming for members of Christ. For if you have been made members of Christ, where then is your head? Members always have a head. If the head had not preceded, the members could not have followed. Where has your head gone? What did you recite in the creed? [We recited that] "he rose from the dead on the third day, ascended into heaven, and now sits at the right hand of the Father." Therefore our head is in heaven.

Consequently, when it is said, "Lift up your hearts," you answer, "We have lifted them up to the Lord." The fact that you have your heart raised up to the Lord is not something you may attribute to your own resources, your own merits, your own efforts, because it is a gift of God to have your heart raised up. Lest you think this, the bishop or the priest who is celebrating the Eucharist continues saying, after the people have answered, "We have lifted them up to the Lord," "Let us give thanks to the Lord our God." Because we have our hearts lifted up, let us give thanks because if he had not given this to us, our hearts would remain earthbound. Moreover, you are personally confirming this by saying, "It is right and just that we give thanks to him" who has enabled us to have raised our heart up to the Lord.

Further, after the sanctification of the sacrifice of God, because he willed that we ourselves be his sacrifice (and this is clearly shown at the moment that this sacrifice is first put upon the altar, the sign of the reality that we are, the sacrifice of God and of ourselves), [the body and blood of Christ] are the sign of the reality that we are. *Therefore when the sanctification of the sacrifice is completed we say the Lord's Prayer, which you have already received and recited.*

Afterwards, this is said: "Peace be with you," and Christians kiss each other with a holy kiss. This is a sign of peace and in the same way as the lips show, it must also happen in the heart, i.e., in the same way as your lips meet the lips of your brother, so your heart should not draw away from his heart.

These are very great sacraments, very great. Do you know in what manner they are recommended? The Apostle Paul says, "Anyone who eats the bread or drinks the cup of the Lord unworthily will be guilty of the body and blood of the Lord" (1 Corinthians 11:27). What does it mean to receive unworthily? To receive it with contempt. So do not let it seem to you as something contemptible. You see it, but what you see passes away. What is signified invisibly does not pass away, however, but is permanent. The bread and wine is received, eaten, and consumed. But surely the body of Christ cannot be consumed? Surely the Church of Christ cannot be consumed? Surely the members of Christ cannot be consumed? Nonsense! Here, as the community of Christ on earth, they will be purified; in heaven they will be crowned. Thus what is signified will remain in eternity. Although it seems to pass away.

Therefore you must receive it [the Eucharist] in this way: You must receive it with yourselves in mind, namely, with unity in your heart and your heart fixed on high. *Your hope must not be for this earth, but for heaven. Your faith must be firmly directed toward God, it must be acceptable to God. What you do not see here, but believe, you will see there, in heaven, where you will rejoice without end.*

Second Sermon: Sermon 272,
In die Pentecostes postremus *(b)* Ad Infantes,
de Sacramento, *vol. 38*[19]

What you see upon the altar of God, you have also seen last night; but you have not yet heard what it was, what it meant, and a great reality the sacrament contained. What we see with our eyes is bread and cup, what your eyes likewise impress upon your mind; but what your faith requires that you learn is that the bread is the body of Christ and the cup is the blood of Christ.

Very briefly, indeed, what has just been said suffices to faith. But faith wants further instruction. For the prophet says: "You will not understand, unless you believe." (Isaiah 7:9). For you can say to me now: "You have commended us to believe, explain it now so that we may understand." For it can happen that the idea could arise in someone's mind: Our Lord Jesus Christ has taken flesh from the Virgin Mary. As a baby he was given the breast, he was nourished, he grew up, and became an adult, suffered persecution, was hung upon a cross, was murdered on a cross, was taken down from the cross, buried, and rose on the third day. He ascended into heaven on the day he wanted. He raised his body up into heaven from where he will come to judge the living and the dead, and he is now seated there at the right hand of the Father. So how can this bread be his body? And the cup, or rather what the cup contains, how can it be his blood?

Sisters and brothers, these things are called sacraments for this reason because in them one thing is seen
and something else is understood. *What you see has a
corporeal form, what is understood has a spiritual fruitful-
ness. If you want to understand the Body of Christ, listen to
the Apostle Paul say to the faithful: "You are Christ's Body
and members" (1 Corinthians 12:27). If therefore you are
Christ's body and its members, your mystery is placed on the
table of the Lord; you receive your mystery. For what you are,
you respond, "Amen," and by responding you commit yourselves to it.* For we hear the words "the body of Christ"
and you answer "Amen." Be a member of the body of
Christ so that your Amen is true.

*But why is this expressed in bread? We do not want to add
something of our own, but let us listen again to the Apostle Paul,
who says this when he is speaking about this sacrament: "We
are one loaf, one body, many as we are" (1 Corinthians 10:17).
Understand and be delighted: Unity, truth, filial love, charity.*

*One loaf: which is this one loaf? [It is the] one body, many
as we are. Call to mind that the loaf is not made out of one
single grain of wheat, but of many. When you are exorcised,
you were, as it were, ground up. When you were baptized,
you were, so to speak, sprinkled. When you received the fire of
the Holy Spirit, it was as if you were baked.* Be what you
see, and receive what you are. (Estote quod videtis, et
accipiter quod estis.) *That is what the Apostle says regard-
ing the loaf. Though he did not say it, he suggested this with
enough sufficiency in telling us what we must understand with
regard to the cup. For in the same way that many grains of*

wheat are moistened into a unity in order that the visible species is formed into a loaf, such is also the case with the wine. Such, too, is what Holy Scripture tells us concerning the faithful: "They were one mind and one heart on the way to God." (Acts 4:32). So, too, with the wine. Brothers, call to mind what wine is made out of: many single grapes on a bunch ground up, but the juice of the grapes is poured together into a unity.

Thus the Lord Christ has also shown us, through signs, that he wanted us to belong to him. He consecrated the mystery of our peace and unity on his table. Whoever receives the mystery of unity and does not hold the bond of peace, does not receive the mystery of his benefit, but receives it as a testimony against himself. . . .

Third Sermon: Sermon Denis 6, 1–3,
Tractatus de sacramentis fidelium,
Dominica Sanctae Paschae[20]

What you see upon the Lord's table, dear sisters and brothers, is bread and wine. But this bread and wine become the body and blood of the Word when a Word comes to them. For the Lord, who was the Word in the beginning, and the Word dwelt with God, and the Word was God, He is the Lord become flesh because of his mercy on account of which he did not despise what he created in his own image. He became flesh and dwelt among us, as you know. For the Word himself became a man, that is, a human soul and the flesh of a man, while remaining God.

*On that account, because he also suffered for us, he com-*mended to us, in this sacrament, his body and blood. Into which he has even made us ourselves as well. And by his mercy, we are what we receive.

Call to mind what this created thing [bread] once was in the field. How the earth brought it forth, the rain nourished it, and ripened it into an ear of wheat and then human labor brought it together on the threshing floor, threshed it, winnowed it, stored it up again, took it out, ground it, added water to it, baked it, and only at that moment made it into the form of a loaf. Call to mind also: you did not exist, you were created, you were brought together to the threshing floor of the Lord by the labor of the oxen, that is, by those who announced the gospel, by their work you have been threshed. When as catechumens you had to wait [for your baptism], you were stored up in the granary. You had given your names [put them on a list for baptism], and you began to be ground by fasting and exorcisms. Later on you came to the water, and you were sprinkled, and you were made one. When the fervor of the Holy Spirit came upon you, you were baked and you were made into the loaf of the Lord.

See what you have received. Just as, therefore, you see that the loaf which has been made is one, so you also are to be one, by loving one another, by keeping one faith, one hope, and undivided love.

When heretics receive this bread, they receive a testimony against themselves because they seek division—while this bread means unity. Likewise the wine was also first present in many grapes and now is one. It is one in the sweetness of the cup, but only after the crushing of the wine press. Likewise after that fasting, after those efforts, after humiliation and contrition, you have come in the name of Christ, as it were, to the cup of the Lord. And there upon the table you are present and you are there in the cup. *Together with us you are this; for together we are this, we drink together, because we live together.*

You will hear now what you also heard yesterday, but today it has been explained to you. Perhaps you kept silent during the response, but yesterday you learned what your reply should be today. After the greeting, which, as you know, is "The Lord be with you!" you heard: "Lift up your heart!" The whole true

Christian life consists in "lifting up our hearts." Not just being Christian in theory, but being Christian in reality and truth consists in this: "To lift up the whole life and heart."

What does it mean to lift up your hearts? Hope in God and not in yourself. You are below, God is above. If you put your hope in yourself, your heart will be below and not above. Therefore, when you hear the priest say, "Lift up your hearts," you reply: "We have lifted them up to the Lord!" Exert yourselves so that you may reply truthfully because you are replying in the presence of the transactions of God. Let it be as you say. It should not be uttered by your tongue, but denied by your conscience. And because he grants you to have your hearts raised up—your own powers are not sufficient for this. Therefore, after you have said that "you have raised them up to the Lord," the priest continues, saying: "Let us give thanks!" What do we give thanks for? Because if we did not have God's grace, we would remain lying on the earth.

Then follows those things that are accomplished in the holy prayers that you will hear so that bread and wine become the body of Christ and blood by the Word. If you take away the Word, you have only bread and wine. Add the Word and you have a sacrament. You say "Amen," and to say "Amen" is to assent to it. "Amen," in Latin, means "it is true."

Next the Lord's Prayer is said, which you have already received and recited. Why is it said before receiving the body and blood of Christ? Because of our human fragility, perhaps our minds imagined something that is not becoming, or we uttered something that should not have been uttered, our eyes saw something that was not decent, our ears heard something exaggeratedly that was not fitting. If perhaps such things have been kept in because of temptation and the fragility of human life, they are washed away by the Lord's Prayer at the moment we say, "Forgive us our trespasses" so that we can safely approach the sacrament. Lest we eat and drink to our own damnation.

NOTES *and* REFERENCES

1. The term *Word* will be capitalized in this section because, here, it refers not just to the simple written word of scripture but to that Word as it is being proclaimed, preached, and celebrated within Christian liturgical gatherings. In this context, like Eucharist, the Word is a sacrament—namely, something tangible that is giving concrete flesh to God.

2. In the Roman Catholic view, Eucharist is more radical than the Word. Indeed the relationship of the Word to the Eucharist might profitably be understood within the metaphor of physical embrace and sexual intercourse (and this may be more than metaphor). The Word is sacramental, but it is less physical than the Eucharist, and the communion it creates is less physical than Eucharistic union. In a manner of speaking, the Word is a preparation for, a readying for, physical union. Its role is to prepare us for consummation. The Eucharist is the touch, the physical coming together, the embrace, the consummation, the intercourse. I suspect that this kind of comparison might scandalize or upset some people. It's pretty earthy, but so

too is the Eucharist. The mystery of the Body of Christ—
God becoming incarnate, Christ leaving us the Word and
the Eucharist, and the intimacy and communion that we
experience with Christ and each other in the Eucharist—
can, in the end, not be exaggerated. Its reality, including its
physical character, goes further than we imagine.

3. Brenda Peterson, *Nature and Other Mothers* (New York: HarperCollins, 1992).

4. Given the earthiness of Christianity, it is not an accident that *carnival* and Mardi Gras, which are, in essence, celebrations of the physical, developed within Christian and particularly Roman Catholic cultures. For a deeper analysis of this, I suggest Charles Taylor, *A Secular Age* (Cambridge, MA: Harvard University Press, 2007), 46–52.

5. Andre Dubus, *Broken Vessels* (Boston: Godine Publishers, 1991).

6. Ibid.

7. G. K. Chesterton, *Everlasting Man* (New York: Dodd, Mead & Company, 1925), 189.

8. C. H. Dodd, *Benefits of His Passion* (Nashville: Abingdon Press, n.d.).

9. Saint Augustine, "Sermon Denis 6," 1–3, in *Tractatus de sacramentis fidelium, Dominica Sanctae Paschae.* (See pages 132–135 for full excerpt.)

10. Frank McCourt, *Angela's Ashes* (New York: Scribner, 1996), 185.

11. Robert Barron, *The Eucharist* (Maryknoll, NY: Orbis Press, 2008), 53.

12. Pierre Teilhard de Chardin, "The Mass on the World," in

Ursula King's *Spirit of Fire: The Life and Vision of Teilhard de Chardin* (Maryknoll, NY: Orbis Press, 1996), 99.

13. Jane Urquhart, *The Underpainter* (Toronto: McClelland & Stewart, Inc., 1997), 95.

14. Gerard Lohfink, "Zur Mögliichkeit Christlicher Naherwartung," in G. Greshake's *Naherwartung, Auferstehung, Unsterblichkeit* (*Quaestiones disputatae* 71) (Freiburg, Germany: Verlag Herder, 1975), 38–81.

15. Saint Augustine, "Sermon 227," in *Die Paschae IV, Ad Infantes de Sacramentis* (see pages 125–128 for full excerpt).

16. 1 John 4, 16.

17. Robert Barron, *The Eucharist*, 10.

18. These homilies from Saint Augustine can be found in most standard compilations of his homilies. However, the particular translations given here are taken from the class notes from the renowned Augustine scholar Johannes Van Bavel and are not found, in this form, in any other printed text. This translation tries to stay close to the original Latin and, at times, sacrifices good grammar for a more accurate meaning. The emphases are my own. As a background to these homilies, I recommend Johannes Van Bavel, *Christians in the World: An Introduction to the Spirituality of St. Augustine* (New York: Catholic Book Publishing Co., 1980).

19. The title of the sermon suggests that it might have been given at Pentecost, but it was more likely given at Easter. It is addressed to "infants," but here the term refers to "infants in the faith," namely, newly baptized adults.

20. A sermon given on Easter Sunday and named after "Denis," the name of the discoverer of this sermon.